a woman's search for worth

Focus on the Family®

a woman's search for worth

Finding Fulfillment as the Woman God Intended You to Be

Dr. Deborah Newman

Tyndale House Publishers, Wheaton, Illinois

A Woman's Search for Worth

ISBN: 1-58997-007-1

A Focus on the Family Book published by
Tyndale House Publishers, Wheaton, Illinois 60189
Renewing the Heart is a registered trademark of Focus on the Family.

Portions of this text were first published as *Then God Created Woman,* 1997, by Deborah Newman, Tyndale House Publishers and Focus on the Family.

Library of Congress Cataloging-in-Publication Data

Newman, Deborah.
A woman's search for worth : finding fulfillment as the woman God intended you to be / Deborah Newman
p. cm.
ISBN 1-58997-007-1
1. Christian women—Religious life. 2. Self-esteem—Religious aspects—Christianity. I. Title.
BV4527 .N49 2002
248.8'43—dc21

2001003995

Editors: Kathy Davis and Liz Duckworth
Cover Design: Candi D'Agnese

Printed in the United States of America
2 3 4 5 6 7 8 9 / 08 07 06 05 04 03 02

To Brian
With love, admiration, and appreciation

Contents

Acknowledgments

I recognize God's faithfulness to me and the vision He has given me for this subject. Since the book *Then God Created Woman* was released in 1997, I have been speaking on the subject of knowing your true identity and worth as a woman. I've met many women who have used the contents of *Then God Created Woman* in Bible study and retreat settings. I wanted to release this material in a context that could be used for personal or group study. Renewing the Heart Ministries and the Focus on the Family creative staff caught my idea and helped me redefine it into the book you now hold in your hands. I want to thank Yvette Maher for her heartfelt leadership in ministry to women. I'm grateful to the brand management team and Julie Küss, specifically, for being so devoted to this concept and product. Mark Maddox has been an encourager and has connected me to the best individuals to shape this work into its potential. I appreciate Kathy Davis for her wise editing and perceptive sensitivity to my foremost responsibilities as a wife and mother amidst the harsh realities of deadlines. Special thanks goes to Liz Duckworth for the final edit.

My husband, Brian, is the key to my successfully finishing a project, as he is so adequate to fill in for me when I need to focus on writing. My children, Rachel and Benjamin, have been helpful and understanding through this whole process. I'm so grateful I have them in my life.

Chapter One

Introduction

Most women accept the subtle messages the world sends us about what we need to be as women—young, sexy, rich, powerful. Others of us try to measure ourselves by certain roles we see outlined in the Bible—submissive, gentle, hospitable. But there is so much more God wants us to experience as women. With this book, I hope to provide you with an anchor for your soul that helps steady you against the world's empty claims to femininity. I want to help you discover that, as a woman, you have unique struggles in this world and your problems have unique answers.

Through the years I've learned there are three areas we must explore on our journey to unmasking and claiming our true feminine identity.

1. We need to understand what makes us tick as women.
2. We need to identify the obstacles that prevent us from seeing what great women we are.
3. We each need to develop a more intimate relationship with God.

These three areas provide the outline for this book.

In all my Christian life and experiences, nothing has been more satisfying, fruitful, and productive for my spiritual life than grasping my true identity. I hope to help you discover your true identity too. I pray that God's message will get deep in your soul, so you can discover the unique design and the beauty you possess as a woman.

In 1 John 1:3-4 (NASB), as John describes why he is writing to the followers, he says:

> What we have seen and heard we proclaim to you also, that you also may have fellowship with us; and indeed our fellowship is with the Father, and with His Son Jesus Christ. And these things we write, so that our joy may be made complete.

I couldn't agree more! When you grasp your true identity, stop condemning yourself and others, and receive the joy, freedom, and pleasure that comes from this, it completes my joy. Oh, and I can't imagine what it does to God's joy!

The Renewing the Heart staff, Focus on the Family editorial team, and I met in beautiful Colorado Springs, Colorado, to discuss the best way to help women grow in their knowledge and experience with God. We discussed women's lives and women's needs. We concurred that there are lots of great Bible studies for women to use in small groups. Some are in-depth, others, very basic. We pondered the vast array of Christian books and resources available on the market today. We found many meaningful and helpful resources that would be difficult to use in a group setting. We recognized that when women meet together in small groups and study material that is thoroughly biblical, their lives are changed. We decided to offer a new product that might fill in the gap of Bible study options—a book, workbook, and Bible study combined to produce a thoroughly biblical examination of a woman's identity in Christ.

That's how *A Woman's Search for Worth* was conceived. Our purpose is to help women grow deeper in their relationships with God. Our hope is that this book will help transform women's lives into images of Christ.

Opening Your Bible, Opening Your Life

There is nothing like opening God's Word and realizing that He is speaking to you, about you, and for you. When you discover that God has a lot to say about you and discover new perceptions about how you can live your life, you have a sense of your true identity. Reading Scripture this way is the purpose of this book. It is written so that you can expose your life to the mirror of God's Word and let Him show you the meaning of your life.

Throughout this book you will find study questions that you are asked to stop and consider before you read on. I suggest that you keep a journal in which you can complete spiritual exercises that are recommended in the book and answer these questions. Your journal can be a beautifully bound book or an inexpensive spiral-bound notebook.

Scriptures are provided for you right in the text along with the study questions. We did this to simplify your life. If you are working on your study on your break at work, or at the park while you watch your children play, you don't have to take your Bible unless it is convenient for you. After each question I provide an answer that you can use for clarification or deeper reflection. If possible, you should complete the chapter and questions before you meet with your group each week. You will get the most out of this study if you take the time to answer the study questions and read God's Word yourself, because it has the most power to transform your life.

Each chapter should take an hour or less to complete. May I suggest that you spend about 10 minutes a day reading the text and answering the questions, rather than trying to carve a large block of time out of your busy schedule.

Group Discussion

This book is written for a woman to read individually or with a group, but I hope you are participating with a group of women. It's great fun to go shopping for a special dress with a couple of girlfriends. Doing this Bible study with some other women will be like that for you. They can point out truths that you didn't notice. They can help you see clearly what God is trying to show you as you share together in His Word. I hope that you will complete this study with a group of women who can encourage you as you grow toward becoming the woman God intends you to be. But if you don't have that opportunity, it's certainly okay to work through the book by yourself.

Leader

It is helpful to have a leader for the group. The leader of the discussion should see herself as a facilitator of the study. She would be in charge of securing a place and time to meet, ordering books, making a schedule including dates by which the chapters are to be read, and so on. There are more suggestions and recommendations for the leader in the appendix.

Discussion Questions

At the end of each chapter there are several discussion questions. These questions are written to help you and your group apply the biblical principles you have studied in the previous week. Most of them don't have right or wrong answers. It is not necessary for you to answer these before you meet with the other women, unless you would like to.

Getting Started

This introduction section is meant to be done during week one of the 11-week Bible study. Today, you are asked to share your answers to the discussion questions that follow. During the week, you are asked to study chapter two. When you return, you will talk about the experiences you have had and the insights you have gained. (If you are doing this study in 10 weeks, simply omit discussion questions for chapter one and move on to chapter two.)

Blessings!
Dr. Deborah Newman
Focus on the Family Author Relations
8605 Explorer Drive
Colorado Springs, CO 80920

Discussion Questions

1. What does the world tell women they need to be? (For example: thin, smart, in charge . . .)

2. What does it mean to you that you are a child of God?

3. When is a time that you most fully experienced God's love for you?

4. If you woke up each morning being fully assured that you were loved, how do you think that would affect your day?

5. How can you claim God's love and your identity in Christ on a practical level? (For example: I wouldn't need to become so defensive when my husband doesn't notice my new hairstyle because I know I matter to God.)

6. Can you think of a woman who seems to grasp her true identity in Christ?

CHAPTER TWO

What Makes Women Tick?

Carrie thought she had made her life what she needed it to be. She grew up in an outlandishly wealthy home with two extremely dysfunctional alcoholic parents. After her father committed suicide when Carrie was 16, her mother married a gold digger who squandered their millions, then left her mother destitute. Carrie hadn't even finished college when she had to drop out and work for the first time in her life. Her waitress job helped support her, while kindhearted relatives took in her mother.

Carrie hated being poor. She was on a quest to become a millionaire again before she was 30. She worked hard to finish her degree and land a good job in New York City, where she met some very influential (and rich) people. She had high standards for the men she would date; they had to come from money, not just be rich now. She needed assurance that the money would never run out.

After Carrie married the man of her dreams, quit her job, and birthed two children, she realized that what she had always thought would bring security didn't bring peace. She still needed something—something money couldn't buy. Carrie's emptiness told her that she hadn't made it after all. Money did not provide the security she sought. Her world felt empty, and she was haunted by unanswered questions about her life.

Like Carrie, many women at some point ask themselves two essential questions: "Who am I?" and "Why am I here?"

- If I were to ask you, "Who are you?" what would you say? In your journal, list the first thoughts that come to your mind. (For example: John's mom, a teacher, a lawyer, a wife, a Christian, and so on.)

My prayer for this book is that God will show you who you really are and that you will discover more accurate answers to these two questions.

In Matthew 16:17-18 (NIV) Jesus tells Peter who he really is.

> Jesus replied, "Blessed are you, Simon son of Jonah, for this was not revealed to you by man, but by my Father in heaven. And I tell you that you are Peter, and on this rock I will build my church, and the gates of Hades will not overcome it."

- Who do you think Peter thought he was before Jesus told him who he really was?

- Who did Jesus say Peter really was?

- Why did Jesus say Peter was here?

If Peter had been asked the question "Who are you?" he may have answered, "I'm a fisherman," or "I'm a husband." Jesus told Peter who he really was. Peter was a rock. He was the rock on which Jesus planned to build His church. Peter was here on earth to build the church of Jesus Christ, and that is exactly what he did. If Peter hadn't let Jesus tell him who he really was and why he was here, perhaps you and I wouldn't have received the message the church was instituted to give. It is because Peter grew to understand who he really was, and why he was here, that you and I have heard the gospel—the message Jesus sent him to share.

Women Look into Mirrors

Women constantly consult mirrors to make sure the images being reflected are suitable to present to the world. Hair perfectly coifed, makeup meticulously applied, clothes ironed and clean, shoes polished. Now we are ready. We have created our image, the image of womanhood.

But this earthly image pales in comparison with the image God holds of us. We often don't recognize that each of us has special features of God Himself inside of us. We focus so much on how we look on the surface that we become oblivious to the most important image, the one that can't be taken away, the one that doesn't turn gray or wrinkle with age.

In Genesis 1:27, God shows us why we are valuable as women:

> So God created man in his own image, in the image of God he created him; male and female he created them.

According to Genesis 1:27, who are you?

Do you understand what it means that you bear the image of God? If you have a personal relationship with God through Jesus Christ, then you are a coheir with Jesus; you are the sister of Christ. If you are Jesus' sister, then you are God's daughter. Since God is the King of kings, that makes you . . . a princess! That's the identity you need to claim. That's who you really are. That's the way God wants you to see yourself. When you know who you really are, you will stop trying to get your identity from other sources.

When you look in the mirror, do you see a woman whose life has been changed by God? A woman who is no longer driven by her insecurities to compete with other women? Are you blessed by who you are? Your search will bring you to a point of embracing the image of God inside you and exploring how to more fully display who God is through the way you live your life.

> [17]I keep asking that the God of our Lord Jesus Christ, the glorious Father, may give you the Spirit of wisdom and revelation, so that you may know him better. [18]I pray also that the eyes of your heart may be enlightened in order that you may know the hope to which he has called you, the riches of his glorious inheritance in the saints, [19]and his incomparably great power for us who believe. That power is like the working of his mighty strength . . . (Ephesians 1:17-19).

In your journal, answer this question: "Why am I here?"

God has specific plans for your life. You are living on the earth at this point in history to experience a glorious way of life, a work that He calls you to do. When you are doing the work that God calls you to do, you won't feel that you are carrying a great burden. He will supply the strength to accomplish what He has chosen for you. Is that the kind of life you want to live?

Eve's Example

The events in Eve's life described in Genesis 1–3 are so radical that we sometimes forget God has more to tell us about her. As the early church writers explored and formulated doctrines, they professed strongly negative thoughts about Eve, based on those passages. Apparently, they didn't spend much time meditating on Genesis 4. When you read that chapter from Eve's perspective, her story emerges as a bittersweet one of faith, hope, and love in the midst of heartache.

In Genesis 4, the focus is on Cain and Abel and their sordid story of jealousy, murder, and sin. We tend to forget that Eve was right there through it all, living the horror. Imagine yourself in her place for a moment. You have two sons, one highly favored of God and another you love just as well, sulky though he may be. Now imagine what happens to a mother's heart when the dark one murders the bright one.

In Genesis 4, every mention of Eve after the Fall shows us how she hung on to her true identity. Although Eve probably longed for a sinless world more than you and I ever would (after all, she lived in one for a time), we don't see her trying to rebuild that world by her own efforts.

There's not a lot written about Eve after Genesis 3, but read the three verses in chapter 4 where her name is mentioned:

> Adam lay with his wife Eve, and she became pregnant and gave birth to Cain. She said, "With the help of the Lord I have brought forth a man." Later she gave birth to his brother Abel (Genesis 4:1-2).
>
> Adam lay with his wife again, and she gave birth to a son and named him Seth, saying, "God has granted me another child in place of Abel, since Cain killed him" (Genesis 4:25).

❧ What do these verses all have in common?

Eve trusted in God for her future. What a tragic existence Eve endured until her death, compared to the life she once knew without sin in the garden. Yet, she is a wonderful example for women to help us discover how we, too, can make it through our personal heartaches and struggles and look ahead with hope.

❧ How did Eve stay in touch with her true image and calling outside the garden?

We can expect that Eve didn't demand love from her husband and children. No doubt she received the love they gave her, but she always relied on her true source of love: her relationship with God. He was the anchor for her soul as she lived in a troubled land.

How do we get to this place of peace where Eve seemed to be? How do we develop such a deep connection to the One who loves our souls that we gain a workable perspective on life and our problems? We begin by seeing how much God loves us. We discover this by looking at Him and not at our circumstances. When we discover God as our living Creator, we discover what can't be taken from us.

Remember Carrie? Her life was dramatically changed when she met God. As a millionaire with a beach house in Florida and a yacht in Maine, Carrie was unsettled by a deep emptiness inside. She finally understood what her father's disappointment with life was all about. A friend introduced her to a personal relationship with God through Jesus Christ. In His love she overcame the hurt from her past. She realized that she craved money so much because it was the only way she'd felt loved and worthy in the past. She forgave her parents for their inability to love her well, and her stepfather for stealing the money her father had earned. In her relationship with God, she found peace that can't be taken away.

Carrie's money has become a source through which she can bless others. She finds she doesn't even want to shop at the same places she did in the past. She can find so many better ways to use her money. She discovered God's love. She looks at the world a whole new way now. She wants to know what God wants for her life.

Why don't we women clearly see what God is calling us to be? Perhaps we are confused about the answer to the question, "What does God really want for a woman?"

❧ What do you think God wants for your life?

Was your answer like any of the following examples: To be somber, not to wear makeup, and to serve others? To always be busy doing things for the church, community, and family? To be a good citizen by being organized, involved, and dutiful? To spend time getting to know Him and discovering how to serve Him? Something else?

These are common ways women think they are fulfilling what God wants for them. But there are two things I know for sure that God wants for us as women. First, He wants us to approach Him with confidence. He also wants us to experience Him as the Creator of our souls. This is quite different from the roles expected of us by the church and society.

Many Christian women try to define and live a religious role when it comes to femininity. They believe that if they focus on being hospitable, quiet, and meek, and doing everything the Bible says a good Christian woman should do, then God will love them. But God doesn't want us to perform for Him. He doesn't want to give us a list of rules, with the promise that if we obey them perfectly, we will get everything we want. Rather, God wants us to get to know Him better, because by doing so we will take on more and more of Christ's characteristics.

Another group of women believes the media's view that women are valuable only if they are young and beautiful. They succumb to almost every message that advertisers offer women. Sex appeal, white teeth, expensive perfume, designer clothes, and carefully applied makeup become indispensable because they tell a woman that she is okay. But God wants us to be discerning about what the world offers us and tells us we need to be.

A third view of what a woman should be is offered by society. A woman's value is in having a career and being independent. Again, God doesn't want us to embrace the rhetoric of society. He wants to give us an anchor for our souls through relationship with Him. Most of all, He wants us to know that we belong—and not just *that* we belong, but *how* we belong.

In Luke 10:38-42, we find a woman named Mary who is an example of a confident woman. In fact, she is even commended by Jesus for discovering what can't be taken away from her. She found what was best about knowing Jesus. Read the passage and contrast the characteristics of Mary and her sister in your journal.

> 38As Jesus and his disciples were on their way, he came to a
> village where a woman named Martha opened her home
> to him. 39She had a sister called Mary, who sat at the
> Lord's feet listening to what he said. 40But Martha was
> distracted by all the preparations that had to be made. She
> came to him and asked, "Lord, don't you care that my
> sister has left me to do the work by myself? Tell her to
> help me!" 41"Martha, Martha," the Lord answered, "you
> are worried and upset about many things, 42but only one
> thing is needed. Mary has chosen what is better, and it
> will not be taken away from her."

We notice that Martha opened her home to Jesus. Martha believed that Jesus was the promised Messiah and that He had come to fulfill God's prophecy. She opened her home because she wanted to share this good news with others.

But compare opening your home to Jesus, as Martha did, to sitting at Jesus' feet and listening to what He said, as Mary did. This was the dramatic difference between Martha and Mary. This contrast made all the difference in understanding Jesus' message and receiving peace from knowing Him.

Another contrast between Martha and Mary is that Martha ended up worried, distracted, upset, and resentful, while Mary found something that couldn't be taken away. Personally, I can relate to Martha's upset, distracted, and worried feelings. I can grasp her resentment of her sister and even of Jesus when she says, "Don't you even care that my sister has left me to do all the work?" I get why she gives Jesus the perfect answer to her problem: "Tell her to help me." What astounds me is Jesus' response to her.

When Jesus responds to Martha, I hear Him also responding to me and all the accusations I bring to Him. I love how Jesus isn't offended by the accusing question. Most of us feel that way about God and Jesus from time to time in our spiritual journeys. God is big enough to handle our anger. He knows we are angry with Him. We won't be able to resolve our anger unless we come to Him and admit it. Like Martha, every time I've been angry with God, I've been wrong. But I'm thankful God receives me the same way Jesus received Martha, showing her the way out of her anger by His love. In this instance, Jesus overcomes her accusation by telling her the truth.

Martha was not wrong for asking for help. She was feeling overwhelmed by the great number of people who were guests in her home. But Jesus does correct her for having the wrong focus regarding God's work. Martha was focusing on the people and all the work that needed to be done. In her worry and distraction she was missing the one thing that was important. When you have that one thing straight, everything else will begin to come together.

- What do you think is the one thing that Jesus wanted Martha to focus on?

Mary found in Jesus the one thing that can't be taken away: a relationship with God. What kept her sitting there at His feet on that hard floor, ignoring the nasty stares of her sister and the judgmental thoughts of others around her? (After all, she was a woman listening to Jesus—something women didn't do in her culture.) It was listening to Jesus and finding the answers to questions she had been asking all her life. It was finding peace and assurance in a relationship with God. It was discovering that the God of the universe took a personal interest in her. It was knowing that God could show her how to live her life in a way that would make a difference for eternity.

We find evidence that Martha responded to Jesus' rebuke. In John 11, after her brother Lazarus died, Martha ran to meet Jesus. She obeyed what He said, even though she didn't understand Him completely. In John 12, where we read that Jesus came to Bethany just before He was crucified, it states that Martha served. She wasn't worried or anxious or resentful. Wish we could say the same about Judas Iscariot, who was a guest at the same dinner. When Martha's sister, Mary, anointed Jesus with costly perfume, Judas complained. There's no complaining from Martha. She got it. She was worshiping through serving. Mary was worshiping by loving. Martha's worship is just as genuine as Mary's because this time it brings peace.

- Do you see God for Who He really is? Do you see yourself the way He sees you? In your journal, write a personal letter to God, inviting Him to help you see who He is and who you are.

Mirror, Mirror on the Wall

What kind of image do you see when you look in the mirror? Do you see a valuable, confident, capable woman? In the power of Christ and through the eyes of the Holy Spirit, you can begin to see your true image in that mirror. You can escape the bondage that prevents you from seeing who you are to God. Let me show you in God's Word what it means to be a woman. Open up your heart and your life to His healing of your femininity. Let's journey together until you can look in the mirror and see for yourself that there is nothing like a woman, and no other woman is quite like you.

- What do you hear God saying to you through what you've read so far?

- What image do you see when you look in the mirror?

Discussion Questions

1. Was it important for Peter to know Who Jesus really was before he could believe what Jesus wanted to tell him about who he (Peter) really was? (Matthew 16)

2. What was Eve's secret to surviving the hard times in Genesis 4?

3. What do you think God wants for women?

4. How is Mary an example of a confident woman? (Luke 10:38-42)

5. What do you think Jesus most wanted Martha to understand? (Luke 10:42)

6. What do you think it means to know your true identity, and how would that change the way you look at life?

Chapter Three

Women, Love, and Relationships

What do you enjoy most about being a woman?

Most women respond to this question by saying they like the depth and warmth, the connectedness, of their relationships. They like that they know what is going on in the lives of their spouses, children, friends, mothers, and others. By and large, women cocoon themselves in an intricately woven fabric of relationships.

As women, we have a lot about which we can be proud. Our lives are full of strength and softness, love and sorrow, laughter and tears, quietness and boldness, hope and courage.

I have an answer to Professor 'enry 'iggins's plaintive question, "Why can't a woman be like a man?" It's because God didn't make her that way, and He had divine reasons for not doing so. God made men and women similar but distinct from each other.

How would you define womanhood? What three or four components of your life most aptly exemplify womanhood?

Most of us define womanhood by our relationships. Our deepest longing as women is to be in harmonious, mutually dependent relationships with humankind. This brings us to our pain. Our deepest pain as women stems from our relationships when we wrongfully presume upon people to give us what only God offers. Our effort to deal with our pain on our own is what creates the messes we face in our lives.

You would never have guessed that what Sylvia wanted most in life was a happy family. Sylvia was a cranky old woman who was always finding fault with everyone—from the way the mailman put the mail in her box to how the grocery store clerk packed her bags. But there was no one she found fault with more frequently than her two grown children and their spouses. Her daughter, JoAnn, was just about ready to completely cut off the relationship with her mom, and her son called her only twice a year. You wouldn't blame Sylvia's children for choosing to distance themselves from their toxic mom. Sylvia's constant criticism and negativity were heavy burdens to bear. Late at night, before she turned out the light for bed, she would cry out to God to make her children like her. Sylvia couldn't see that her criticism was pushing them away. She thought she was helping them to be better people. She simply could not comprehend why her children were so distant.

How do you feel about yourself right now? Do you like who you are? Are you basically content with life and happy to get up in the morning? If you answer yes, I bet you are content with most of your relationships. If we feel good or in control or needed, then our problems seem few.

I can speak from my own experience. I find that my own relationships tug so deeply at my soul that I often view my image and value as a woman by the quality of my earthly loves. That's why I try to get people to like me. I don't want to feel rejected. If I'm loved, I feel lovable. If I'm treasured, I feel valuable. I believe that these feelings are common to women. But the glow from being loved and valued in our earthly relationships fades. Somehow there isn't enough there to sustain us and restore our souls. As women, we must first recognize how much our relationships influence our view of ourselves, and then find the sources of our negative images.

God Created Women with Unique Relationship Needs

Genesis 1 describes the creation of Adam and Eve as a single, unique event. It states that man and woman were both created in God's image. They were both blessed and charged with ruling the creatures of the earth, as well as producing offspring. But that isn't where the story ends. Genesis 2 has some amazing and exciting information about creation. In this chapter, God takes a breath and says, "Hold on, world, there are some specifics I've got to let you in on. This stuff is just too good to keep to Myself. Are you ready to hear it?" Then He moves on with the rest of the story.

In order to understand how we are driven by love and relationships, it is important for us to look at how God created us. He is the creator of our bodies and our souls. He put us together just right. We'll get a better picture of that process if we compare the differences in the creation and curses of both men and women.

The Creation and the Curses

Read Genesis 2:5-7, the creation of man.

> [5]And no shrub of the field had yet appeared on the earth and
> no plant of the field had yet sprung up, for the Lord God had
> not sent rain on the earth and there was no man to work the
> ground, [6]but streams came up from the earth and watered the
> whole surface of the ground—[7]the Lord God formed the man
> from the dust of the ground and breathed into his nostrils the
> breath of life, and the man became a living being.

Now read Genesis 2:18-25, the creation of woman.

> [18]The Lord God said, "It is not good for the man to be
> alone. I will make a helper suitable for him." [19]Now the

> Lord God had formed out of the ground all the beasts of
> the field and all the birds of the air. He brought them to
> the man to see what he would name them; and whatever
> the man called each living creature, that was its name. [20]So
> the man gave names to all the livestock, the birds of the
> air and all the beasts of the field. But for Adam no suit-
> able helper was found. [21]So the Lord God caused the man
> to fall into a deep sleep; and while he was sleeping, he
> took one of the man's ribs and closed up the place with
> flesh. [22]Then the Lord God made a woman from the rib
> he had taken out of the man, and he brought her to the
> man. [23]The man said, "This is now bone of my bones and
> flesh of my flesh; she shall be called 'woman,' for she was
> taken out of man." [24]For this reason a man will leave his
> father and mother and be united to his wife, and they will
> become one flesh. [25]The man and his wife were both
> naked, and they felt no shame.

- What differences do you note in how the two were created?

- From what were they created? (2:7; 2:22)

Man was created from the dust of the ground. The woman was created from the rib of the man. The creation of man and woman were unique from each other. After the man was created, he opened his eyes and the first thing he saw was God; the second thing he saw was the garden. When the woman was created, she opened her eyes and the first thing she saw was God; the second thing she saw was Adam.

Now read Genesis 3:16-19.

> [16]To the woman he said, "I will greatly increase your pains
> in childbearing; with pain you will give birth to children.
> Your desire will be for your husband, and he will rule over
> you." [17]To Adam he said, "Because you listened to your

> wife and ate from the tree about which I commanded you, 'You must not eat of it,' "Cursed is the ground because of you; through painful toil you will eat of it all the days of your life. [18]It will produce thorns and thistles for you, and you will eat the plants of the field. [19]By the sweat of your brow you will eat your food until you return to the ground, since from it you were taken; for dust you are and to dust you will return."

How was the man cursed? (3:17-19)

How was the woman cursed? (3:16)

Do you notice a pattern here? I see a very clear explanation of the differences between men and women before and after the Fall. Before the Fall, the first mention of a man is in the context of cultivating plants—making things happen. He was created from the dust, and after the Fall, was cursed by his inability to make things happen like he could before. Now he would have thorns and thistles to deal with.

Likewise, the woman was first spoken of in the context of relationship. She was created because man needed a relationship. She was created from the living rib taken from the man. She was cursed in the area of her relationships—pain in childbirth and discord with her husband. Notice that when Paul gives us God's instructions about marriage in Ephesians 5:33, he talks to a man about loving his wife—meeting her core need for relationship. He speaks to a wife about respecting her husband—meeting the man's core need to feel capable. In Genesis 1–2, we see our deepest longing for relationship.

Read Genesis 2:24-25 once more.

> [24]For this reason a man will leave his father and mother and be united to his wife, and they will become one flesh. [25]The man and his wife were both naked, and they felt no shame.

What characterizes the kind of relationship Adam and Eve enjoyed?

The essence of a man and woman's relationship is mutual dependence and oneness. Even Adam and Eve's nakedness went beyond the physical. They were naked spiritually and emotionally as well as physically. They were completely exposed to each other—body, mind, and soul—and completely accepting of each other. Their differences didn't divide them. Rather, their differences became the foundation for their oneness. The fact that we were created for oneness helps us understand what is really going on in our souls as we live outside the garden. It helps us see what is at the bottom of the messes we live in.

Genesis 3 Reveals Where Relationships Went Wrong

How we were created and cursed teaches us a lot about how we can live. In fact, Genesis 3 helps us to discover where our problems come from.

Read Genesis 3:1-9.

> 1Now the serpent was more crafty than any of the wild ani-
> mals the Lord God had made. He said to the woman, "Did
> God really say, 'You must not eat from any tree in the gar-
> den'?" 2The woman said to the serpent, "We may eat fruit
> from the trees in the garden, 3but God did say, 'You must
> not eat fruit from the tree that is in the middle of the gar-
> den, and you must not touch it, or you will die.' " 4"You
> will not surely die," the serpent said to the woman. 5"For
> God knows that when you eat of it your eyes will be
> opened, and you will be like God, knowing good and evil."
> 6When the woman saw that the fruit of the tree was good
> for food and pleasing to the eye, and also desirable for gain-
> ing wisdom, she took some and ate it. She also gave some
> to her husband, who was with her, and he ate it. 7Then the
> eyes of both of them were opened, and they realized they

> were naked; so they sewed fig leaves together and made
> coverings for themselves. [8]Then the man and his wife heard
> the sound of the Lord God as he was walking in the garden
> in the cool of the day, and they hid from the Lord God
> among the trees of the garden. [9]But the Lord God called to
> the man, "Where are you?"

❧ Why do you think the serpent, who was so crafty, talked to the woman alone?

❧ How did the serpent get the woman to doubt God?

Satan's Strategies

Satan had two strategies to turn Adam and Eve from God, to get them to destroy their perfect world and create the mess you and I now live in. First, he chose to divide and conquer. He spoke to the woman first, because engaging both of them would have been more difficult. Second, he caused them to doubt God's word and character.

❧ Compare the woman's understanding of what God said in Genesis 3:2-3 with what God actually said in Genesis 2:16-17.

> [16]And the Lord God commanded the man, "You are free
> to eat from any tree in the garden; [17]but you must not eat
> from the tree of the knowledge of good and evil, for when
> you eat of it you will surely die."

❧ Are there any differences?

❧ Why did the woman eat the fruit? (v. 6)

Eve did not have a clear understanding of God's instructions indicated by her misquoting God to Satan. She ate the fruit because she was deceived by what she saw—fruit that was good to eat, and by what she heard from Satan—eating the fruit would make her wise.

- Who was with Eve when she ate?

- Why do you think Adam ate the fruit?

- When were their eyes opened? (v. 7)

- What was the most immediate result of sin? (v. 7)

- After Adam and Eve hid from each other, what did they do next? (v. 8)

- What happened to their relationships with God after they sinned? (v. 8-9)

The difference between how Adam and Eve were tempted was that Satan spoke directly to Eve, distorting God's word, whereas Adam was tempted indirectly through watching Eve's actions. He ate after it appeared nothing had happened to Eve. They responded individually for different reasons to the temptation.

Though they acted individually when they sinned, they experienced the result of their sin—guilt and shame—together. The first blast of sin-scarred reality (the one you and I know too well) was experienced in the context of their relationship when they tried to hide by covering their nakedness with leaves. Alienation, the opposite of oneness and unity, was the most immediate effect of sin.

Adam and Eve had experienced God in a unique way. For a while, they had enjoyed a perfect relationship with Him, a relationship in which their soul hunger—their innate need to relate do someone greater than themselves—was fully satisfied. They saw how God had made everything in their world to please them. And yet, at the point they chose to eat the fruit, they doubted God's goodness. They were questioning God's motives and character. Was he holding out on them, denying them something wonderful and godlike, as Satan suggested? They, like Satan before them, sinned because they wanted to be like God.

- What do you learn about God by how He responded to these two sinners in verses 7-9?

- When did He come?

- What did He say?

- Does He seem to be a vindictive, angry God?

In Genesis 3:9, God stepped in to deal with the mess the man and woman had created. He didn't jump down and deliver His just blow the minute they sinned. He didn't react the way I sometimes do when I discover one of my son's infamous messes (mud tracked from the backyard straight to where he sits in front of the TV) and ask, "Why did you do this? What were you thinking?" No, God came as He always had, in the cool of the day. When God found the man and woman trying to hide from Him in the bushes, He didn't laugh. He responded as a respectful parent, pretending not to notice them hiding like cowards. He simply called them by name and waited for the two to reveal themselves.

When the man and the woman finally emerged, God continued to treat them with respect, asking Adam, "Who told you that you were naked? Have you eaten from the tree of which I commanded you not to eat?" (Genesis 3:11, NASB). Again, God's mercy and patience are evident. It's like catching your child with his hand in the cookie jar and allowing him to admit the guilt rather than jumping ahead to a punishment. Well, Adam knew he was caught, but instead of repenting, he placed blame.

> [10]He answered, "I heard you in the garden, and I was afraid because I was naked; so I hid." [11]And he said, "Who told you that you were naked? Have you eaten from the tree that I commanded you not to eat from?" [12]The man said, "The woman you put here with me—she gave me some fruit from the tree, and I ate it." [13]Then the Lord God said to the woman, "What is this you have done?" The woman said, "The serpent deceived me, and I ate" (Genesis 3:10-13).

❧ Who do Adam and Eve blame for their choice to sin?

In the midst of all this sin and destruction, we see the character of God illustrating His great love for us. Now that we get to the curses, we witness an even more profound revelation of His love and character. Both the man and the woman sinned, both hid from each other and from God, and both blamed someone else for their sinning. (Eve blamed the serpent; Adam blamed Eve and God.) But when God talked to them, He addressed them separately.

> [14]So the Lord God said to the serpent, "Because you have done this, "Cursed are you above all the livestock and all the wild animals! You will crawl on your belly and you will eat dust all the days of your life. [15]And I will put enmity between you and the woman, and between your offspring and hers; he will crush your head, and you will strike his heel" (Genesis 3:14-15).

❧ What is the unique and specific information about life outside the garden given to us by the God who designed us?

❧ What does God say to the serpent?

To the serpent, He laid it on the line. The serpent went from being the craftiest of created beings to the most humble and hated of beasts. Triumphantly, God let Satan know where he was headed. From the woman would come a seed—the first mention of Christ! God's pronouncement on the serpent went right to the point: "I'll take care of you now, and I'll finish with you later by the seed of the woman you deceived."

> To the woman he said, "I will greatly increase your pains in childbearing; with pain you will give birth to children. Your desire will be for your husband, and he will rule over you" (Genesis 3:16).

❧ What does this mean for the woman?

The woman was cursed in the area of her relationships. The change in the relationship with her man and the realities of the differences in their body types and reproductive abilities would leave her in a position to experience discord rather than instant love. A woman's relationship pain would surface in a fallen world since men are stronger, do not carry the burden of reproduction, and are driven to achievement more than relationship. Her pain would stem from the fact that her relationships would not be what her soul longed for them to be.

Read Genesis 3:17-19.

> 17To Adam he said, "Because you listened to your wife and
> ate from the tree about which I commanded you, 'You
> must not eat of it,' "Cursed is the ground because of you;
> through painful toil you will eat of it all the days of your
> life. 18It will produce thorns and thistles for you, and you
> will eat the plants of the field. 19By the sweat of your brow
> you will eat your food until you return to the ground,
> since from it you were taken; for dust you are and to dust
> you will return."

❧ What does this mean for the man?

The most painful realities for the man were in the area of his adequacy—his limited ability to evoke from the ground what he needed for life. He would confront constant obstacles as he labored to meet the needs of himself and others. The result was a sense of inadequacy—his deepest pain.

History has confirmed the truth of the curses: Men and women perceive reality differently. Women are more relationship-oriented and men are more achievement-oriented. This is why God addressed the man and the woman separately, even though they were affected by each other's curses. The life of toil ending in death directed to the man (Genesis 3:19) applied to the woman as well. Otherwise, women would not die. The curses describe the painful realities men and women would face as fallen persons.

Do you now understand the source of your pain? Do you see how God made you for relationship? Knowing this doesn't diminish the trauma of your pain or provide a magic cure. But it does give you a connection to God. It helps you see that He knows the messes in your life. These messes can drive you to God or away from Him.

Read Genesis 3:21. Describe what happened.

> The Lord God made garments of skin for Adam and his wife and clothed them.

God was the one who shed the first blood in the garden. He killed an animal and made clothing for the two. God knows that fig leaves aren't going to cut it in life outside the garden. God's love exposes more than just their need for more covering and protection. Do you see this as a picture of what Jesus does for us? His shed blood makes it possible for us to wear His robes of righteousness. Again, it was God who sent Jesus to shed His blood for us. Can you imagine a God who loves and cares for you more? But that's not all. Look at how God loves the two sinners.

> [22]And the Lord God said, "The man has now become like one of us, knowing good and evil. He must not be allowed to reach out his hand and take also from the tree of life and eat, and live forever." [23] So the Lord God banished him from the Garden of Eden to work the ground from which he had been taken. [24]After he drove the man out, he placed on the east side of the Garden of Eden cherubim and a flaming sword flashing back and forth to guard the way to the tree of life (Genesis 3:22-24).

❦ Why does God banish them from the garden, and what efforts does He make to assure that they don't get back in?

God expels them from Eden to protect them. He's not mad at them and punishing them. He just knows them. He knows that they will be tempted to eat of the Tree of Life. That would have been Satan's only hope. If he could have gotten them to eat of the Tree of Life, we would be doomed as sinners forever, just like Satan.

❦ Read Revelation 22:14 to more fully understand God's desire for us.

> Blessed are those who wash their robes, that they may have the right to the tree of life and may go through the gates into the city.

❦ When does He want us to eat of the Tree of Life?

God can't wait for us to eat of the Tree of Life. But it is only for those who become completely His through Jesus Christ. I am looking forward to eating from that tree.

❦ How does Proverbs 14:12 define our problem?

> There is a way that seems right to a man, but in the end it leads to death.

We think we know what is best to do about our lives and our relationships. We end up wanting the wrong things. This was Sylvia's problem.

She could identify that she was in pain. She knew that all she wanted was children who loved her and felt happy in her presence. She could not grasp that her negative and critical comments toward her children drove them away from her. She justified her criticisms as part of her "job" to make her children better people.

God heard Sylvia's prayers for good relationships with her children. After the pastor at her church preached about family relationships, Sylvia made an appointment to receive counsel from him. Her pastor skillfully and tactfully helped Sylvia see her side of the problem. He encouraged Sylvia to write letters to each of her children and their spouses expressing her longing to be close to them. He told her to include the reasons that she was proud of them and to offer them genuine encouragement about themselves. In response, her daughter came over to give her a hug, and her son called the same day he received the letter.

As women, we are all longing for perfect relationships with God and each other. Nothing is more soothing to our souls than to love and be loved. But our sin gets in the way. We need to trust God to show us a better way in all our relationships.

Discussion Questions

1. What do you think is most unique about the way God created woman?

2. What made the difference between how Adam and Eve responded to temptation and how Jesus responded to temptation? What applies to your life from these examples?

3. What are some of the kindnesses God bestowed on Adam and Eve after they sinned?

4. Why do you have problems today?

5. Where do you find rest?

6. What does God want for you?

Chapter Four

Becoming a Woman

Jinny was anything but confident. She tried attending a variety of women's groups in her search to belong, hoping someone would notice her and become her friend. If anyone did talk to Jinny, she became so self-conscious that she could hardly look that person in the eye. When she tried to share prayer requests for her son and family, she spoke too softly and quickly, overwhelmed with anxiety about speaking in public. Jinny's life and relationships were a complete mess. The only identity she claimed was that of a weak failure, someone of little use to God.

Along our journey to becoming women, we often lose sight of who God made us to be, just as Jinny did. We don't see ourselves as His unique creations, complete in Him. Rather, we see ourselves as unsightly creatures with big hips and wrinkled faces, and we feel useless and worthless. How did we get that way? What interferes with being able to see ourselves as God sees us?

- What influences can you name right now that affect the way you see yourself as a woman (the media, ex-boyfriends, sexual abuse as a child, comments made by a father or brother)?

Before eye color is determined or personality unfolds, before race becomes detectable, even before the single-celled fertilized egg divides, a person's gender has been established. And at the time of birth, it is the one point of reference everyone attributes to a human being. Gender is the initial identity given to a newborn. "It's a girl!" and "It's a boy!" are statements that will shape a child from the first seconds of birth to the grave. Those exuberant shouts will determine a great deal about how a child will be perceived by others and what she will believe about herself.

These perceptions and beliefs are influenced by parents, society, and church. They each contribute to a woman's female identity. A mother sets the example of femininity, while a father's role is to demonstrate how a girl's femininity is valued. Ideally, he does this by treating his daughter and other women with respect and appreciation. Society sets expectations about sexual identity, often based on stereotypical gender roles. The church influences a girl's sexual identity in the way it portrays God—either accurately, as a loving Father, or inaccurately, as a demanding oppressor.

Jinny's story is a textbook example of a woman with a sexual identity crisis. Her parents were strong and loving, but they didn't prepare her for what the world was really like. They made every decision for her and treated her like a china doll. The only time she rebelled in any way was when she chose the man she would marry. Her parents weren't completely happy with her choice, but her mom got caught up in giving her a beautiful wedding and seemed to deny the issues that didn't seem right.

Her parents ended up being correct about Michael. He abused Jinny physically in the early years of their marriage and didn't hold a steady job for years. But Jinny never let on to her parents what kind of pain she was enduring in her marriage.

Jinny didn't get much affirmation about herself from the world or society. She chose to be a stay-at-home mom and received little approval for that decision. Her younger son adored her, but that didn't boost her confidence when she was out in the world. Yet something kept drawing her back to church. Whenever life with Michael seemed overwhelming, she prayed. She knew that her only hope for love and confidence was in a personal relationship with God, but she didn't know how to grow close to God, in part because of her failure to develop a healthy sexual identity.

Jesus: The Perfect Example of Healthy Sexual Identity

If we want a picture of perfect sexual identity, we need to look at Jesus Christ. While God is neither male nor female, when He was made flesh, His flesh was male. Let's look closely at Jesus' example of healthy masculinity. From His example, women can learn more about how to embrace healthy femininity.

Read the following references to Jesus' life as they relate to His masculinity.

1. Mark 10:2-12

> 2Some Pharisees came and tested him by asking, "Is it law-
> ful for a man to divorce his wife?" 3"What did Moses
> command you?" he replied. 4They said, "Moses permitted
> a man to write a certificate of divorce and send her away."
> 5"It was because your hearts were hard that Moses wrote
> you this law," Jesus replied. 6"But at the beginning of cre-
> ation God 'made them male and female.' 7'For this reason
> a man will leave his father and mother and be united to
> his wife, 8and the two will become one flesh. So they are
> no longer two, but one. 9Therefore what God has joined
> together, let man not separate." 10When they were in the
> house again, the disciples asked Jesus about this. 11He
> answered, "Anyone who divorces his wife and marries
> another woman commits adultery against her. 12And if she
> divorces her husband and marries another man, she com-
> mits adultery."

2. John 19:26

When Jesus saw his mother there, and the disciple whom he loved standing nearby, he said to his mother, "Dear woman, here is your son . . ."

3. Luke 8:1-3

[1]After this, Jesus traveled about from one town and village to another, proclaiming the good news of the kingdom of God. The Twelve were with him, [2] and also some women who had been cured of evil spirits and diseases: Mary (called Magdalene) from whom seven demons had come out; [3]Joanna the wife of Cuza, the manager of Herod's household; Susanna; and many others. These women were helping to support them out of their own means.

4. Luke 3:22

And a voice came from heaven: "You are my Son, whom I love; with you I am well pleased."

5. Matthew 13:55

"Isn't this the carpenter's son? Isn't his mother's name Mary, and aren't his brothers James, Joseph, Simon and Judas?"

Now match the passages above to the appropriate descriptions of how Jesus modeled healthy masculinity.

_____ A. Jesus was a son and brother.

_____ B. Jesus welcomed women followers to come along with the chosen disciples.

_____ C. Jesus listened to the voice of His Father in heaven.

_____ D. Jesus fulfilled His responsibilities as the oldest son in making arrangements for His mother.

_____ E. Jesus had a high regard for women. His teaching on divorce was to protect women from being thrown out in the street for any reason a husband cared to think up.

Although we don't know a lot about the first 30 years of Jesus' life, we do know that He lived His life in a healthy way. He grew to manhood and fulfilled the responsibilities that were given to Him. He took on His father's trade as a carpenter. Before His death, He made arrangements for His mother to be cared for. He responded to God's call to spread the Word to all people and left the trade of His earthly father to take on the vocation given to Him by His heavenly Father.

You see His healthy sexual identity when you study His treatment of women: in the way He encouraged Mary for sitting and listening to His teaching (Luke 10:42), in His teaching on divorce (Mark 10:2-12), in His welcome of women followers (Luke 8:1-3). Perhaps the most compelling evidence of God and Jesus' high regard for women is that it was women who were the first to witness the greatest event in human history—the resurrection of Jesus (Mark 16). This is even more compelling when you realize that women weren't even considered credible witnesses in that time.

Read Luke 2:52.

> And Jesus grew in wisdom and stature, and in favor with God and men.

- In what four ways did Jesus mature?

- How have you matured in these four ways?

- In which area do you need to grow most?

Jesus grew mentally, physically, socially, and spiritually. These are areas that we need to grow in as well.

The Development of Healthy Femininity

Jinny's relationships with her parents taught her she needed them to make every decision. They didn't teach her to be a self-confident woman. This is probably what drew Michael to her in an unhealthy way. Jinny was easy to manipulate and put down. He felt in control when Jinny was the victim—a role she had learned as she passed through various stages of development.

A normal, healthy process of developing female identity involves several stages. You probably passed through each of these stages without even thinking about how they influenced you. That's why it is important to reflect on your life. In doing so, you may identify wrong beliefs you developed about your sexuality that keep you from embracing the healthy feminine identity God offers you.

The Eight Stages of Development

To help us identify the obstacles to developing a healthy feminine identity, I've divided a woman's life into separate stages of development and raised issues at each stage that will guide us in our discussion of how to become the women God intended us to be. As you answer the questions that follow each stage, think about each stage in your own life and identify the influences on your own concept of femininity.

A special note: Many women report they have no memory of childhood. This is common. Sometimes these women do not want to remember one or more traumatic events (such as sexual molestation, an abusive childhood, or exposure to traumatic events such as the death of someone close or war). They unconsciously erase all memory in an effort to protect themselves from pain, despair, and hopelessness. When I talk to women who have no childhood memories, I suggest that they pray, asking God to reveal to them what they need to remember in order to grow. If you're suicidal, depressed, have an eating disorder, or suffer from other emotional problems, it might be time to consider past issues that may be haunting you in the present. If you are suffering from any of these problems and do not have a counselor to work through them with you, please call Focus on the Family at 800/AFAMILY and ask for the counseling department.

The following passages and questions will help you recall messages you received as a child that may be keeping you from enjoying the freedom God longs for you to have today.

Stage One: Ages 1–2—I am a girl. A healthy feminine identity for a young child at stage one is exhibited as she is appropriately attached to her parents or caregivers. This means that a child has opportunities to be loved—held, fed, and nurtured—by both her mother and her father. This lays the foundation for the child to believe that she is loved for who she is.

❧ How do you think your parents felt about you as a girl?

❧ Did you have a safe environment to live in?

Stage Two: Ages 3–5—I want to be like Mommy. During stage two, a child begins to experience firsthand that she is a girl and that her interactions with the world are greatly influenced by this fact. From which public restroom to use, to what kind of haircut to get, a young child starts to notice many differences between males and females, not the least of which are sexual characteristics.

A girl who manages this stage successfully is able to identify male and female differences without putting more value on one than the other. The preschooler will notice that women wear makeup and men shave their faces, but it doesn't mean one is superior to the other; they are simply different.

❧ Who were your male and female role models at this stage?

❧ How did you accept the world you lived in at this stage? Were you happy?

Stage Three: Ages 6–10—I want to be like the other girls. In general, a girl's self-esteem is relatively intact at this stage. Girlhood is often characterized by hope and adventure as girls focus on discovering how they fit into the world. A girl with a healthy sense of self by age 10 will have several girlfriends, share a close relationship with her mother, and enjoy special conversations with her father. She can understand the concept that God loves her, her sins separate her from Him, and Christ's death brings her back into relationship with Him. During stage three, a girl is eager to explore the world and discover all the new and exciting opportunities that await her.

❦ Who were your girlfriends at this stage?

❦ What did you like most about yourself at this stage?

❦ What were you most afraid of?

Stage Four: Ages 11–13—I am a woman-girl. This stage of becoming a woman creates an eruption in every aspect of a girl's life. Her body is changing; her friends are changing; her relationships with her parents and with boys are changing. She is leaving a carefree world of petty disagreements with girls and occasional antagonism toward boys for a world where her worth is partly determined by how appealing she is as a woman.

Indications of a healthy passage through stage four of feminine sexual development are a young woman's acceptance that her life has changed and her willingness to take greater responsibility for her own thoughts and actions. During this stage, a girl begins to lose her innocence and her belief that the world was designed to bring her happiness. She learns to accept that conflicting emotions, opinions, and actions are a part of her struggle to develop her own identity. A strong feminine identity is exhibited as the preteen recognizes her differences but does not see them as flaws and does not allow her femininity to hold her back.

❦ Who was your best friend during this stage?

❦ What were you like during these years of storm and crisis?

❦ What was your relationship with your parents like?

- How did you feel about your changing (or not changing) body?

- How did boys treat you?

Stage Five: Ages 14–18—I must not be like my mother. Every healthy girl rebels to some degree. If a mother or father is too enmeshed and too controlling with a daughter, it prohibits separation and hinders the daughter's maturity. At stage five, it is healthy for girls to take a long, close look at their mothers and decide to form their own ideal of womanhood. An adolescent girl's major task is to develop a sense of identity apart from those of her parents. She will also be able to respect her parents, even if her values and goals differ from theirs.

- Did you rebel against your parents at this stage?

- In what way were you most determined not to become like your mother?

- What kinds of experiences did you have with boys, and how did they affect how you saw yourself at this stage?

Stage Six: Ages 19–29—I have both male and female characteristics. By this stage, a healthy woman has developed confidence in her sexual identity. She has become more comfortable in her womanly form. In her confidence, she becomes willing to step out of roles and peer definitions to discover who she really is. She observes both male and female characteristics in her personality and develops strengths in both areas. It is during this stage that most women make critical decisions about marriage and career.

- Did you find that your image of yourself as a woman further developed during your young adult years? In what ways? How did you view yourself?

- How did marriage or vocation influence your image of yourself as a woman?

Stage Seven: Ages 30–50—I am my mother. During this stage of womanhood, we begin to understand our unique gifts and influences on the world. When we don't run from our femininity but truly value it and ourselves, we discover how we are equipped differently from men to make the greatest impact on our world.

Between the ages of 30 and 50, we are challenged to evaluate ourselves in a new way because, when we look in the mirror, we are often literally looking into the faces of our mothers. For most of us the earliest memories we have of our mothers were when they were about these ages themselves. Their identity and ways of life subtly influenced us, even when we found ourselves separated from them by distance or death.

- When did you first realize that you are like your mother in certain ways?

- How has your mother influenced your life positively or negatively?

Stage Eight: Ages 50 and up—I am a woman. A woman with a healthy feminine identity at this stage will thoroughly enjoy life, despite our society's view that an older woman lacks value. Her strong sense of identity upon entering middle age enables her to view menopause as an accomplishment rather than a loss. She will also develop a brighter vision of who God wants her to become in the years remaining to her, because she will know that as long as she is on His earth, God has a purpose for her. A woman with a healthy feminine identity at this stage lives with confidence that she is deeply loved and deeply valuable to God and others.

- What are you contributing to the world at this stage of life?

❧ What do you hope to be doing 10 years from now?

Whatever stage of womanhood we are in, there are always exciting, challenging, and painful realities to face. It's when we stop moving forward, stop recovering from the crises, and stop grieving our losses that we get stuck with a shallow definition of feminine identity. We'll think femininity is what we look like or how many Bible studies we have done or how much we can accomplish. This keeps us searching for fulfillment in the wrong ways, which leads only to despair. It's like aimlessly drifting away from home.

God longs for each of us to develop into a woman not only physically but also emotionally, with confidence and a strong sense of identity. He boldly tells us in Romans 8:29 that He predestined us to grow into the form and likeness of Jesus Himself. Even in a fallen world, we are in the process of becoming the women God longs for us to be. We were each designed to reflect our Creator in unique ways that glorify Him and give us peace.

❧ Why don't we have confidence as women?

Many of the negative experiences we had during our years of maturing brought us condemnation. Jesus came to bring us confidence. John 3:17-18 reveals God's plan. He didn't come to condemn us. He knows that we are condemned already. The question is: Will we receive the light Jesus brings, or would we rather spend our time on earth in darkness (John 3:19-21)?

❧ List ways you have learned to condemn yourself. (For example: It's my fault that my sister and mother aren't talking.)

❧ List ways others have condemned you, such as names called, ridicule, and so on.

All of us have experienced painful events and relationships that have led us to speculate that we may not be worth much. The truth is that we are women made in God's image. If we really believed and lived this truth, we would have a confidence that defies worldly reason, for even if we aren't specially talented, rich, famous, or beautiful, we are His.

Lasting confidence is developed through a relationship with God and leads to a life that no longer clings to abilities, fame, possessions, or beauty. We need to stop looking in the wrong places to find fulfillment and happiness. When stripped of worldly things we are left to look within ourselves, and there, with the right light, discover that it is a relationship with God that soothes a hurting soul. God's hope for us is that we develop into confident women through our relationships with Jesus Christ.

> 12In him and through faith in him [Jesus Christ] we may approach God with freedom and confidence (Ephesians 3:12).

- Are you a confident woman?

- Refer back to the lists you made above about ways you condemn yourself and ways others condemn you. Cross off anything on that list that God doesn't condemn you for.

- Is there anything left?

- Are you sure that God condemns you for it?

- If yes, confess your sin to God.

> If we confess our sins, he is faithful and just and will forgive us our sins and purify us from all unrighteousness (1 John 1:9).

❧ Now cross off everything that has been forgiven by God.

One day at Bible study a confident woman, Loretta, took Jinny by the arm and asked to pray with her. Loretta wasn't put off by Jinny's tears about her marriage and her despair over her rebellious oldest son. She listened to Jinny's heartaches. She encouraged Jinny to keep up with the Bible study lessons and to attend regularly. Jinny met God on a deeper level through those experiences. She developed the confidence to lovingly confront Michael about their marriage. He agreed to go to a marriage enrichment event with her, where they learned communication skills. The confident relationship she built with God helped strengthen her other relationships and helped her grow toward becoming the confident woman God designed her to be.

Discussion Questions

1. How did Jesus treat women?

2. How did Jesus model healthy masculinity?

3. What is healthy femininity?

4. Where does our condemnation come from?

5. How can we be confident women?

6. What is the greatest truth you've learned about women?

Chapter Five

Receiving God's Love

So far we've discovered how important relationships are to women. God offers us relationship and complete love, yet somehow we struggle to receive this love. It doesn't make sense. What keeps us from enjoying and fully receiving a love relationship with God?

Deena always wanted to know God. She kept reading books, attending seminars, praying with friends—all in an effort to know Him. One month she spent over $250 on books and tapes about knowing God. It was the cry of her heart, but somehow all her efforts and pursuit only made her feel more distant from Him.

God created us in His image, and a significant component of that image is a desire to love and be loved. God would never allow us to be born with a need without providing for it. In fact, He is the only One who can truly satisfy our need. First John 4:8 says, "God is love." God defines Himself as love. Again in 1 John 4:19, we are told, "We love because he first loved us." God has done everything possible to provide for our love need, though this is sometimes hard for us to see. Our deepest need for love has been provided by God though

Jesus Christ. "In this is love, not that we loved God, but that He loved us and sent His Son to be the propitiation for our sins" (1 John 4:10, NKJV).

There is nothing God wants more than for us to respond to His love. God desires a relationship with us because He loves us. And He knows that when we respond to His love for us and begin to love Him back by trusting His Word and doing as He wants, we will find soul contentment. Some of us will find financial success, some fame, others healthy and long lives. These are all nice benefits, and they are certainly God-given. But they aren't guaranteed for every child of God. What God promises each one of us, and what cannot be taken away, is a soul linked to Him through love.

In Luke 3:22, God announces to the world His pleasure in Jesus with these words: "You are My beloved Son, in You I am well pleased" (NKJV). He feels the same about you and me. We are His beloved daughters. We are a precious part of His universe, a part He cannot bear to be without.

Read the following Scripture passages.

> How great is the love the Father has lavished on us, that we should be called children of God! And that is what we are! (1 John 3:1)
>
> This is how God showed his love among us: He sent his one and only Son into the world that we might live through him. This is love: not that we loved God, but that he loved us and sent his Son as an atoning sacrifice for our sins (1 John 4:9-10).
>
> We love because he first loved us (1 John 4:19).
>
> The Lord is not slow in keeping his promise, as some understand slowness. He is patient with you, not wanting anyone to perish, but everyone to come to repentance (2 Peter 3:9).

[16]"For God so loved the world that he gave his one and only Son, that whoever believes in him shall not perish but have eternal life. [17]For God did not send his Son into the world to condemn the world, but to save the world through him. [18]Whoever believes in him is not condemned, but whoever does not believe stands condemned already because he has not believed in the name of God's one and only Son" (John 3:16-18).

❧ In your journal, write the love God is expressing in each scripture, personalizing it to yourself. Here's an example:

1 John 3:1. Debi, God has the greatest love there is and He lavishes it on you, completely coating your entire being in His love when He claims you as His own child. Do you realize who you really are? You are His daughter!

Now, it's your turn.

What Keeps You from Receiving God's Love?

Scripture gives us a picture of God's wise, tough, exuberant, determined love. Though the truth of God's love is clear in Scripture, we still have a difficult time accepting it. Sometimes the distance from the head to the heart is great. What keeps us from responding to this deep and abiding love?

There is an art to having a mutual love experience with our Creator. His kind of love is literally out of this world. The love or fulfillment we experience from parents, men, success, and fame doesn't come close.

❧ How has God proven His love for you?

❧ What does it mean for you to love God?

[28]One of the teachers of the law came and heard them debating. Noticing that Jesus had given them a good answer, he

> asked him, "Of all the commandments, which is the most important?" [29]"The most important one," answered Jesus, "is this: 'Hear, O Israel, the Lord our God, the Lord is one.
> [30]Love the Lord your God with all your heart and with all your soul and with all your mind and with all you strength.'
> [31]The second is this: 'Love your neighbor as yourself.' There is no commandment greater than these" (Mark 12:28-31).

❧ What is the most important thing in the world?

> The Lord delights in those who fear him, who put their hope in his unfailing love (Psalm 147:11).

❧ How does God respond when we love Him back?

The first time I felt God's love in a deep way I was 18 years old and 3,000 miles away from my family and friends. I had been hurt and rejected in a relationship and was preparing to spend the summer ministering to students. I told my parents I would phone them when I arrived at my destination, but because of the time difference and a late-night meeting I had to attend, I missed my chance to call them before they went to bed. I set my alarm for the middle of the night to catch them before they left for work the next morning. My timing was wrong, and I woke them too early. After a short conversation, I said good-bye so they could go back to sleep. Feeling that I had disappointed everyone, I went back to bed.

Completely alone, I lay there unable to stop my tears of grief. Suddenly, I sensed God's invitation to allow Him to hold me. I distinctly remember turning over in my bed and feeling His arms around me, an assurance that it would be okay. The next morning, I read Psalm 34:18, which says God is close to the brokenhearted. I envisioned Him holding me in His arms, close to His heart. It was the first time I received God's love in the deepest recesses of my soul.

That experience was similar to the many times I have comforted my children through ear infections, broken bones, or skinned knees. The fact that I am there hugging them does not change the circumstances of their pain, but it does change their perspective on it. Whereas they once felt hurt and alone, they now feel comforted and loved.

Why We Resist God's Love

Unfortunately, we resist God's perfect love, which makes it difficult or impossible to escape the cycle of damaging relationships. There are three resistances we need to overcome in order to prepare our hearts to truly receive God's love. Consider how your attitudes and actions stand in your own way as you read each of the following passages.

Resistance 1: We don't want to see ourselves as we really are. To paraphrase Luke 7:36-48, "He who is forgiven much is loved much." We can't really experience how much we are loved until we understand how much we have been forgiven. Only when we see ourselves as we really are will we be able to understand the depth of God's love for us. We cannot come into the presence of God without being aware of our sin—which is probably one of the reasons we stay away. The prophet Isaiah said that he saw the Lord high and lifted up. His most immediate reaction to this sight was to call himself a man of unclean lips and say that he lived among a people of unclean lips (Isaiah 6:5). When you really see God for who He is, you suddenly become aware of your own sinfulness. It's this deep awareness of your sinfulness in the presence of His holiness that reveals the depth of His love.

> Dear friends, let us love one another, for love comes from God. Everyone who loves has been born of God and knows God (1 John 4:7).

❧ Do you regularly confess your sins to God?

We can't grasp the fullness of God's love until we grasp the fullness of our own sinfulness. But we wholeheartedly resist this because we know that if we see ourselves as we really are, we will want to run and hide, just as Adam and Eve did.

Picture this. It's Saturday morning, and you're trying to catch up on all those messy jobs you didn't do during the week. You're in your grubbiest clothes and you smell like a thoroughbred after a race. Your face is covered with grime and your hair looks like a windswept haystack. You're scrubbing the toilet when you hear the doorbell ring. Muttering under your breath, you swing the door open to find the new pastor and his wife, or your best friend's mother who is dying to meet you, or the person you've just started dating or want to date. . . . Not a pleasant scenario, is it? A person who should be seeing you at your best has found you . . . well, at your worst instead.

Now let's picture that person waiting to be invited into your house anyway. You hesitate, unwilling to let him or her bask in your uncleanness, as it were. You expect the person to stammer, "Oh, I see you're busy," and beat a hasty retreat. That's human. And yet, if that someone saw (and smelled!) you at your worst and still wanted to spend time with you, you would be justified in believing that he or she was quite willing to accept you in spite of the mess.

God is at home in us in spite of the cobwebs and dirt that we don't see (Jeremiah 17:9-10). He comes in, longing to see us clean up the grime and appear the way He designed us, but He is never unwilling to be there with us, right in the middle of our messes.

To overcome resistance 1, we must allow ourselves to be embraced by God even in the midst of our messes.

Resistance 2: We try to earn a love that is freely given. We are loved, and when we truly love, our love is a response to this reality and not a way to get love. Love that is earned is not love at all. We don't earn God's love; He gives it to us.

> This is love: not that we loved God, but that he loved us and sent his Son as an atoning sacrifice for our sins (1 John 4:10).

❧ What do you do that makes God love you the most?

Relationship with God is about being, not doing. God is more concerned that we be in a relationship with Him than that we perform for Him. This is so far from our human experience it seems unnatural.

I must confess that too many things I've done in the name of loving God have nothing at all to do with loving Him. Rather, they are my feeble attempts to prove myself worthy of His love.

What happens to you when someone shows you kindness? Do you want to slap that person in the face? No, you want to return the favor by being kind. When you feel loved by God, you will want to love Him back by serving Him.

We are given a great example of this in Luke 7:37-38. A woman came to Jesus and anointed Him with costly perfume and washed His feet with her tears. This wasn't an effort to earn love. Her behavior was motivated by a heart so moved by His love for her that this was the best way she could express the joy in her soul. It was a completely selfless expression. She wasn't saying, "Notice me! I'm doing a good thing for You." She was saying, "Thank You! I feel so loved by You that I want to return that love."

To overcome resistance 2, we must bask in the reality of God's love and see our service and obedience as nothing but the natural outpouring of a soul that is deeply loved.

Resistance 3: We fear the unknown. We deeply resist not having a pseudo sense of control in our lives. I say "pseudo" because our fear of the unknown stems from the fact that we think we can control this world. But can we really? I heard a preacher say once that life on earth is like riding mules: We get on thinking we are in control, but we are not. Life is stubborn and often takes us places we would rather not go.

> There is no fear in love. But perfect love drives out fear, because fear has to do with punishment. The one who fears is not made perfect in love (1 John 4:18).

- What is the one thing you are most afraid God may ask you to do?

We not only fear letting go of control, we also fear relating to God. After all, He is Spirit. We aren't as sure of ourselves and our relationships when we don't have flesh and blood before us. We aren't sure we are hearing Him right or experiencing Him right.

To overcome resistance 3, we must enter fully into God's embrace so that our fears melt away. It is only in believing that we are loved with an everlasting love that we begin to leave our fears behind and experience great joy at the thought of getting to know our Creator better.

- List the three resistances in your journal, then under each, list ways in which you find yourself resisting God's love.

- Can you think of any other reasons that you might resist God's love?

Steps to Receiving God's Love

The great spiritual task before us is to honestly believe and receive God's enormous love for us. Here are four ways you can open yourself more to receiving God's love.

1. Identify your image of God. My image of God as a teenager was that of an old man in the sky with a whip, ready to come down any time He saw me having fun.

- What is your image of God?

- How do you think God wants you to see Him?

- Do you need help breaking through your mistaken image of God? Ask God to reveal to you how He really is.

2. Open yourself to God's love and forgiveness in brokenness and without false guilt. As we saw earlier, one of the resistances to receiving God's love is our effort to earn love rather than opening up to God. Too many people have tried to earn God's love because they feel overwhelmed and doomed by guilt. Usually, the guilt they are feeling is not true guilt. God gives us guilt out of His kindness to us. God's guilt is a life-giving, energizing guilt.

What keeps you from God? Are you letting Satan block you by his constant accusations? Believe that there is no condemnation to those who are in Christ Jesus. Be courageous and open your heart to Him.

> Or do you show contempt for the riches of his kindness, tolerance and patience, not realizing that God's kindness leads you toward repentance? (Romans 2:4)

❧ Why does God want us to feel conviction over our sin?

> [8]Even if I caused you sorrow by my letter, I do not regret
> it. Though I did regret it—I see that my letter hurt you,
> but only for a little while—[9]yet now I am happy, not
> because you were made sorry, but because your sorrow led
> you to repentance. For you became sorrowful as God
> intended and so were not harmed in any way by us.
> [10]Godly sorrow brings repentance that leads to salvation
> and leaves no regret, but worldly sorrow brings death.
> [11]See what this godly sorrow has produced in you: what
> earnestness, what eagerness to clear yourselves, what
> indignation, what alarm, what longing, what concern,
> what readiness to see justice done. At every point you
> have proved yourselves to be innocent in this matter
> (2 Corinthians 7:8-11).

❧ Is it possible to feel a sadness about our sins that doesn't come from God?

- Compare the characteristics of godly sorrow and worldly sorrow from this passage.

3. Keep pursuing God. Many women tell me that they try to know God, but they just can't.

- What do the following Scripture passages say about finding God?

> [11]"For I know the plans I have for you," declares he Lord, "plans to prosper you and not to harm you, plans to give you hope and a future. [12]Then you will call upon me and come and pray to me, and I will listen to you. [13]You will seek me and find me when you seek me with all your heart. [14]I will be found by you," declares the Lord, "and will bring you back from captivity" (Jeremiah 29:11-14a).

> "If my people, who are called by my name, will humble themselves and pray and seek my face and turn from their wicked ways, then will I hear from heaven and will forgive their sin and will heal their land" (2 Chronicles 7:14).

These two passages are promises that if we seek God, He will reveal Himself to us. This does not mean that we will get instant answers or instant relief. It is our consistent desire to see Him for Who He is that clarifies our vision of Him.

Begin pursuing God right now by asking Him to show Himself to you. When I was 15 years old, I was rebellious and running from God. It was at a Christian camp that I first sensed that I was missing out on something. I can't remember any particular person who inspired me through words or example to want to know God. I think I was affected more by the general atmosphere at the camp. I sensed that God was as real as a dear friend and that He wanted the best for my life.

During the few minutes alone in my cabin, I spoke out loud: "God, it seems that some people here know You in an exciting way. I would like to know You that way too." Then I jumped off my bunk to live my life as I always had. But by slow increments, God began to change me. He had me spend the whole summer away from my friends. I read a Christian book, and the camp counselor gave me a piece of notebook paper with some verses on it to read. I have been reading my Bible daily ever since.

If you seek Him, you will find Him.

4. Pray and listen. Prayer is our communication with God. The Bible is full of individuals' conversations with God. When Jesus came, He opened a whole new dimension of prayer for us. No one had ever dared to call God "Abba"—Daddy God. It is when we see God the Creator as God our loving, caring Daddy that our communication becomes an intimate interaction.

- Close this lesson by writing a prayer in your journal to your Daddy God—Abba Father.

Praying and listening to God is really quite simple. Talk to God, read His Word, listen in prayer. Remember that a one-way conversation (you listing all your requests) doesn't promote intimacy. Understand the dynamics of allowing a two-way relationship to develop. Be quiet in God's presence; let Him speak to your heart; let Him lead you to His Word, where He will show you His thoughts and instructions. Time, prayer, and listening will lead you to God so He can guide you on your journey.

Once we start listening to God, we will discover that He has much to say to us about the relationships that tug so deeply at our souls. In fact, He is the only One who can heal the damage caused by our relationships. The healing begins through forgiveness. We'll go there next.

Discussion Questions

1. How do you know that God loves people?

2. How do you know that God loves you?

3. Why aren't more Christians focused on and satisfied in God's love for them?

4. In what ways do you resist God's love?

5. How has your image of God changed over time?

6. Why does God want to claim us as His children?

Chapter Six

The Healing Power of Forgiveness

When Jesus' disciples asked Him to teach them to pray, part of the prayer He taught them included a daily accounting of how sin affects our relationships. Matthew 6:12 says, "Forgive us our debts, as we also have forgiven our debtors." He even went further in His teaching on forgiveness to say, "For if you forgive men when they sin against you, your heavenly Father will also forgive you. But if you do not forgive men their sins, your Father will not forgive your sins," (Matthew 6:14-15). Forgiveness is very important to God.

Why is our God, who is so extremely merciful and kind to us, so adamant about the need for forgiveness, both in our relationship with Him and our relationships with others?

Who thought up forgiveness? Walter Wangerin calls forgiveness a "divine absurdity."[1] I like this definition for two reasons. First, the word divine is well-chosen, since no human would have ever conceived of forgiveness. It is a gift given to us from God. Second, the word absurdity is so fitting when you think of forgiving a person who has committed a heinous act against you.

Before I ever forgave others or helped individuals learn to forgive, I always thought forgiveness granted all the benefits to the offender. In the process of struggling with forgiveness, I have found that it is my own soul that receives the greatest benefit from it. I have witnessed amazing changes in people through the healing power of forgiveness. I've seen people become free from panic disorders, suicidal depressions, and bulimia, each through the doorway of forgiveness. Bitterness is replaced by love, joy, and laughter; a life is freed up to enjoy relationships with God and others.

Lee Ann suffered from terrible panic attacks. It took several trips to the emergency room to convince her that her anxiety was the cause of her heart problems. She began taking an antianxiety medication, and the panic attacks were more controllable. Her doctor recommended that she also attend counseling sessions. She told Lee Ann that if she resolved some of her pent-up emotions, she might even become free of panic attacks completely. Lee Ann agreed to give it a try. In counseling she dealt with many painful memories and emotions related to her alcoholic mother. The counselor helped her forgive her mother. The result was just as Lee Ann's doctor had predicted. After forgiving her mother, Lee Ann was able to stop taking her medication and live a life free of panic attacks.

Read the parable Jesus told in Matthew 18:21-35.

> 21Then Peter came to Jesus and asked, "Lord, how many
> times shall I forgive my brother when he sins against me?
> Up to seven times?" 22Jesus answered, "I tell you, not
> seven times, but seventy-seven times. 23"Therefore, the
> kingdom of heaven is like a king who wanted to settle
> accounts with his servants. 24As he began the settlement, a
> man who owed him ten thousand talents was brought to
> him. 25Since he was not able to pay, the master ordered
> that he and his wife and his children and all that he had

> be sold to repay the debt. [26]"The servant fell on his knees
> before him. 'Be patient with me,' he begged, 'and I will
> pay back everything.' [27]The servant's master took pity on
> him, canceled the debt and let him go. [28]"But when that
> servant went out, he found one of his fellow servants who
> owed him a hundred denarii. He grabbed him and began
> to choke him. 'Pay back what you owe me!' he demanded.
> [29]"His fellow servant fell to his knees and begged him, 'Be
> patient with me, and I will pay you back.' [30]"But he
> refused. Instead, he went off and had the man thrown
> into prison until he could pay the debt. [31]When the other
> servants saw what had happened, they were greatly dis-
> tressed and went and told their master everything that had
> happened. [32]"Then the master called the servant in. 'You
> wicked servant' he said, 'I canceled all the debt of yours
> because you begged me to. [33]Shouldn't you have had
> mercy on your fellow servant just as I had on you?' [34]In
> anger his master turned him over to the jailers to be tor-
> tured, until he should pay back all he owed. [35]"This is
> how my heavenly Father will treat each of you unless you
> forgive your brother from your heart."

- Record your thoughts and feelings in your journal. Write down how you would feel if you were the following characters:
  - the king who was owed 10,000 talents (millions of dollars)
  - the servant who owed 10,000 talents
  - the servant who owed a hundred denarii (a few dollars)

- What do you think Jesus was trying to teach by this story?

Peter had asked Jesus how many times he should forgive someone who sinned against him. He had already caught on that Jesus' teaching about the law was much more intense than that of the religious leaders of the day, especially when it came to the laws governing relationships.

Therefore, Peter felt quite generous when he suggested the answer to his question, "How many times should we forgive a brother who has sinned against us?" by estimating seven times. (The religious leaders of that day said you should forgive a person three times.) Our ways are not God's ways! Our instincts tell us that forgiving people who have sinned against us will leave us victims of sin, not victors. Jesus' answer shocked Peter and the rest of us when He said, "Not seven times, but seventy-seven times."

Jesus wasn't saying that you should count up the times you forgive others until you reach a certain number. He was saying much more. He was saying that you can't even ask a question like that if you fully understand what it means that God has forgiven you. So, in Jesus' custom, He told them a story—the parable you just read. I think Jesus was teaching that we are totally absurd when we refuse to forgive our brothers. No one feels that a servant who has been forgiven millions should go to his fellow servant who may owe him a few bucks and demand payment. When you completely grasp what Jesus did for you through His work of forgiveness on the cross, you won't be fooling around taking petty accounts of who has forgiven whom and when. You will want to forgive.

Jesus not only taught about forgiving those who sin against us, He also demonstrated forgiveness. In the following passages, whom and for what sins did Jesus forgive in each?

> 2Some men brought to him a paralytic, lying on a mat.
> When Jesus saw their faith, he said to the paralytic, "Take
> heart, son; your sins are forgiven." 3At this, some of the
> teachers of the law said to themselves, "This fellow is blas-
> pheming!" 4Knowing their thoughts, Jesus said, "Why do
> you entertain evil thoughts in your hearts? 5Which is eas-
> ier: to say, 'Your sins are forgiven,' or to say, 'Get up and
> walk'? 6But so that you may know that the Son of Man
> has authority on earth to forgive sins. . . ." Then he said
> to the paralytic, "Get up, take your mat and go home."

[7]And the man got up and went home (Matthew 9:2-7).

[44]Then he turned to the woman and said to Simon, "Do
you see this woman? I came into your house. You did not
give me any water for my feet, but she wet my feet with
her tears and wiped them with her hair. [45]You did not give
me a kiss, but this woman, from the time I entered, has
not stopped kissing my feet. [46]You did not put oil on my
head, but she has poured perfume on my feet. [47]Therefore,
I tell you, her many sins have been forgiven—for she
loved much. But he who has been forgiven little loves little."
[48]Then Jesus said to her, "Your sins are forgiven."[49]The
other guests began to say among themselves, "Who is this
who even forgives sins?" [50]Jesus said to the woman, "Your
faith has saved you; go in peace" (Luke 7:44-50).

[3]The teachers of the law and the Pharisees brought in a
woman caught in adultery. They made her stand before
the group [4]and said to Jesus, "Teacher, this woman was
caught in the act of adultery. [5]In the Law Moses commanded us to stone such women. Now what do you say?"
[6]They were using this question as a trap, in order to have
a basis for accusing him. But Jesus bent down and started
to write on the ground with his finger. [7]When they kept
on questioning him, he straightened up and said to them,
"If any one of you is without sin, let him be the first to
throw a stone at her." [8]Again he stooped down and wrote
on the ground. [9]At this, those who heard began to go
away one at a time, the older ones first, until only Jesus
was left, with the woman still standing there. [10]Jesus
straightened up and asked her, "Woman, where are they?
Has no one condemned you?" [11]"No one, sir," she said.
"Then neither do I condemn you," Jesus declared. "Go
now and leave your life of sin" (John 8:3-11).

> Jesus said, "Father, forgive them, for they do not know what they are doing." And they divided up his clothes by casting lots (Luke 23:34).

> [39]One of the criminals who hung there hurled insults at
> him: "Aren't you the Christ? Save yourself and us!" [40]But
> the other criminal rebuked him. "Don't you fear God," he
> said, "since you are under the same sentence? [41]We are
> punished justly, for we are getting what our deeds deserve.
> But this man has done nothing wrong." [42]Then he said,
> "Jesus, remember me when you come into your kingdom."
> [43]Jesus answered him, "I tell you the truth, today you will
> be with me in paradise" (Luke 23:39-43).

Jesus forgave a paralyzed man (Matthew 9:2-7), a prostitute (Luke 7:44-50), a woman caught in adultery (John 8:3-11), those who crucified Him (Luke 23:34), and the criminal who was crucified with Him (Luke 23:39-43), in addition to many others, including you and me. Jesus taught about forgiveness, modeled forgiveness, and invites us to live a life of forgiveness because He loves us.

Each of us has been hurt by our relationships. We women are in particular need of fully understanding the realities of forgiveness because we are more connected in relationships and therefore we have more hurt from our relationships. When we are hurt in relationships, what is the first thing we want to do? We either plot to get revenge or we want to withdraw and deny the reality of what happened.

> "The Spirit gives life; the flesh counts for nothing. The words I have spoken to you are spirit and they are life" (John 6:63).

❧ What happens if we forgive in the flesh? In the spirit?

Betty Ann Smith was an amazing Bible teacher. She was one of those women you would call a pillar of the church. Each weekday morning, she led 100 women into the mysteries of the Bible. She was a loving and caring Christian woman. That's why no one was more amazed than Betty Ann when she realized that she really had not forgiven her mother.

Betty Ann's mother, Susan Davis, suffered from bipolar disorder. When Betty Ann was a teenager, she was humiliated by her mother's cyclical bouts of mania. Her mother would lose touch with reality and end up downtown preaching in the rain on the street corner. The most humiliating incident was when her mother was found naked and drunk in their neighbor's backyard.

It was tough on Betty Ann to grow up feeling totally motherless. Deep in Betty Ann's heart she had buried the hateful words and accusations her mother made against her. One night, after Betty Ann returned from youth group, her mother chased her around their house with a hairbrush, accusing Betty Ann of having sex with a boy. Betty Ann's mother finally got so bad that she was committed to a mental health facility. This brought both relief and shame to Betty Ann.

By the time Betty Ann realized that she hadn't forgiven her mother, Mrs. Davis had been dead for nearly 20 years. It was during a spiritual retreat that Betty Ann's defenses were broken. The Holy Spirit helped her recognize the deep resentment she harbored against her mentally ill, dead mother. You see, Betty Ann would never allow herself to admit that she was angry with her mother. How could she? Her mother suffered from a mental illness. Still, Betty Ann had been sinned against. Those sins needed to be forgiven.

During the part of the retreat in which participants were asked to hammer nails in a cross, Betty Ann began to experience forgiveness in her spirit. It was a tangible representation identifying with Christ's forgiveness and the need to forgive others. All those years when she thought she had forgiven her mother, she had simply felt pity for her. Pity and forgiveness are two entirely different things. Betty Ann felt a freedom at the age of 56 that she had never experienced before. She discovered the true healing power of forgiveness.

Because forgiveness is one of the most misapplied of the Christian doctrines, let's review now what forgiveness is not and what it is.

What Forgiveness Is Not

Forgiveness is not forgetting. There were many times when Betty Ann could forget the numerous tormenting experiences she had with her mom, but that didn't mean she had forgiven her. I challenge you to find the verse that says "forgive and forget" in your Bible. Get a concordance and try to find it. It won't be there.

I will always remember the most significant experiences of forgiveness in my life. These memories are of spiritual victories whereby God overcame the fear, rage, and resistance created in my soul by another person's actions toward me. In true forgiveness, I release my hatred, self-protection, and desire for vengeance, but I keep all of my short- and long-term memories. When we've experienced the healing power of forgiveness, we never forget the release we feel in our souls. Through forgiving, we are able to forget "what lies behind" and reach forward to "what lies ahead" (Philippians 3:13), which involves letting go of the pain and being freed from hatred, fear, and bitterness. We remember those painful circumstances in a way that gives us hope for the future. True forgiveness gives us back our lives.

Forgiveness is not masking hurt. When we are sinned against, we hurt. Our instincts tell us to control the hurt. Many of us are pros at denying our hurt. We think that is forgiveness, but it's not.

- Did Jesus mask His hurt from the sins that were committed against Him?

> [2]Let us fix our eyes on Jesus, the author and perfecter of our faith, who for the joy set before him endured the cross, scorning its shame, and sat down at the right hand of the throne of God. [3]Consider him who endured such opposition from sinful men, so that you will not grow weary, and lose heart (Hebrews 12:2-3).

- How does God's Word describe Jesus' hurt?

When Jesus hung on the cross, He died for every sin you and I will ever commit. Second Corinthians 5:21 says that He became sin for us. Our Savior didn't smile and say, "Oh, they really aren't that bad." No, He was deeply and completely acquainted with our wretchedness. That was the only way He could forgive us for everything. We can't forgive a transgression if we won't let ourselves face how angry, hurt, and betrayed we feel because of the offense.

Forgiveness is not an emotion. After we've been hurt, we want to feel better. Many of us try to use forgiveness as a feeling to make us happier. Betty Ann did this for 30 years. She read about forgiveness, and she tried to forgive in the flesh so she could replace her hurt with forgiveness.

> Jesus said, "Father, forgive them, for they do not know what they are doing." And they divided up his clothes by casting lots (Luke 23:34).

- Is Jesus expressing a good emotion here?

- What is Jesus experiencing—an action or a feeling?

Forgiveness is not an action we take without agony of the soul. It is not easy to do. For me, forgiveness begins as a decision to trust God, rather than a desire or feeling of wanting to be close to the person who has offended me. My emotions toward the person may be completely antagonistic, but that doesn't affect my decision about forgiving that person.

Forgiveness is not necessarily reconciliation. Could Betty Ann be reconciled with her mom? Of course not, her mother was dead. It is quite possible that, if her mom were alive and Betty Ann told her mom that she forgave her, she might have become enraged. The great thing about forgiveness is that we are free to forgive each and every person who has ever sinned against us. Forgiveness doesn't depend on reconciliation. We are told to forgive even though we may not be reconciled to the person we are forgiving.

> "For God so loved the world that he gave his one and only Son, that whoever believes in him shall not perish but have eternal life" (John 3:16).

- Who does God love?
- Who is God willing to forgive if that person believes in Jesus Christ?
- Who will be reconciled to God?

As Jesus hung on the cross and shed His blood on our behalf, He was willing to forgive the sins of every person who has been or ever will be born. But He certainly has not been reconciled to everyone. He's only been reconciled to those who are willing to admit their need for forgiveness. In the same way, reconciliation can be experienced only when offending parties are willing to admit their actions.

It is freeing to know that our part of forgiveness doesn't depend on the response of the offender. However, reconciliation does depend on the offender. Reconciliation is possible only when the forgiver and the person being forgiven can come to terms about the offense.

Forgiveness is not revictimization. Many people are afraid of forgiveness because they think it means they will become the victims of the persons who have sinned against them. This is not what Jesus teaches.

True forgiveness cleanses a heart of the damage caused by an offense. In the process of forgiveness, we realize the need for boundaries—decisions we make about our relationship to the offender that prevent the relationship from being unhealthy, that prevent us from being revictimized. Boundaries are knowing what we are responsible for. Jesus forgave the murderous Pharisees who sought to catch Him. But on numerous occasions He slipped away (John 5:13; 7:1; 7:30) because it wasn't God's plan for Him to be killed yet. When God asks you to forgive others who have offended you, He is not asking you to be a victim. Being a victim and forgiving are two totally different things.

- Who has hurt you most deeply?
- Do you feel you have forgiven that person?
- Did you recognize in yourself any of the characteristics of false forgiveness?

It is easy to practice false forgiveness, but there is nothing less satisfying to the soul. One day I thought I would save money by buying a different sliced cheese. I didn't realize when I picked it up that it was imitation cheese. It didn't go over too well with the family, so it was a total waste of money. Likewise, we can waste a lot of time, effort, and energy buying into false forgiveness.

While jogging at five in the morning, I tripped on an uneven sidewalk and fell flat on my face. I skinned not just my knees but my hand and shoulder as well. It gave me a whole new compassion for my children when they come to me with their skinned knees. As the scabs were forming, it seemed like forever until I had new, healed skin. One day, though, the skin that once was torn and bruised had turned fresh and pink. Healing wasn't instantaneous or without scars, but it happened. Forgiveness heals the wounds in our souls in much the same way. What does it mean to truly forgive? Let's take a look at the positive side of forgiveness now.

What Forgiveness Is

Forgiveness is a process. Perhaps God is speaking to you through this study about a person you need to forgive. You can begin the process of forgiveness today, but that doesn't mean you will instantly feel the freedom of complete forgiveness.

For deep offenses, it may take years to experience the full freedom of forgiveness. I compare forgiveness to peeling layers off an onion. You can dig deeply and take off many layers at once, but there are lots of thin layers as well, which makes forgiveness a process of patiently addressing the issues that come up.

- Is God speaking to you about forgiving a certain person?

- Are you willing to commit to the process?

Committing to the process means admitting that you are powerless to forgive on your own. You are telling God that you want Him to forgive in you. You are willing to begin, knowing it may take years before you feel the complete release of God's work of forgiveness in your heart.

Forgiveness is a decision. The most important contribution you make in the process of forgiveness is to trust God enough to make the decision to forgive. In human matters, forgiveness comes down to a decision. It is a decision to trust that God knows more than you do and that forgiving the person who hurt you will heal you.

- Are you willing to choose God's plan for forgiveness? Do you believe that God loves you and that is why He is teaching you about forgiveness?

George MacDonald said, "It may be infinitely less evil to murder a man than to refuse to forgive him. The former may be the act of a moment of passion; the latter is the heart's choice."[2] No one can force us to forgive, and no one can keep us from forgiving. Forgiveness is a decision to trust not our own instincts but the voice of God. When I have decided to forgive, it was not because the offender asked me to do so or even acted in a way that created a desire in me to forgive. I forgave because I trusted that God loves me and that He would never tell me to do something that wasn't good for me.

Forgiveness is desiring reconciliation. You can use this act of forgiveness as a litmus test to determine how far along you are in the process of forgiveness. As God cleanses our souls from bitterness and hatred, He replaces them with love. As forgiveness does its work, you move from being an obsessed, embittered woman to a willing agent of God's love. The reconciliation that you desire is evidence of the changes going on in your heart through forgiveness. Desiring reconciliation means that you are willing to be reconciled to the one who offended you if that person is willing to accept responsibility for his or her actions. When you are reconciled to God, it is easy to see whose actions are right and whose are wrong. When it comes to our human relationships, the lines are not so clear. Perhaps the person we are forgiving and seeking reconciliation with doesn't see things the same way we do. But for reconciliation to take place, there must be an openness in the hearts of both parties to admit wrong and come to a mutual understanding.

- Envision the person you are forgiving asking for forgiveness and reconciliation. Are you willing to let that person back into your life?

Forgiveness is alchemy for the soul. True forgiveness brings about a seemingly magical transformation. Whereas we were once burdened, consumed, and obsessed, now we are transformed, free, and willing. When I was 16 years old, I read a quote that has had a great impact on the way I have lived my life: "I will never allow another person to ruin my life by making me hate him."[3] God has used these words to keep my soul free from the burden of hate. Hate creates chemical reactions in our bodies. Unresolved hatred and anger have been linked to heart disease and burnout. A soul that is free of hate through forgiveness goes through a chemical transformation. Forgiveness is definitely an internal transformation, as we are cleansed of hatred and bitterness.

> Have you ever felt the unburdening power of forgiveness? How long was it from the time you chose to forgive until you felt this freedom?

Steps to Forgiveness

There are no "six simple steps to forgiveness." But I have seen myself and others go through stages. Here are three stages of the forgiveness process that have helped guide people through the path of forgiveness.

1. Fully examine the wrong. A lot of us don't experience the full healing power of forgiveness because our spirituality won't allow us to feel the anger that is stored inside. Ephesians 4:26 says to be angry and sin not. Anger in itself is not sin. It is what we do with our anger that makes it sin. I find it helpful to express the anger in my soul in a letter that I don't send to the person who offended me. This helps me fully recognize the reality of who and what God is asking me to forgive.

> On a separate piece of paper or in your journal, write a letter expressing your anger to the person you need to forgive.

2. Confess your own sins. How have you allowed the sin committed against you to influence you to sin? Have you been angry at God? Have you developed a life of hate and anger? Have you become afraid to live? Have you not loved well? Have you been afraid to love God? It is important for you to honestly admit your own sins and take responsibility for your own life in the process of forgiveness.

> Take some time to consider your own heart and confess to God any sins that you are responsible for.

3. Commit to the process of forgiveness. Now it's time to let God do what only He can do. Forgiveness in the Spirit is a spiritual process. He can reach and cleanse places in your soul that you could never touch. It's time to trust God and let Him free you from the bondage of unforgiveness.

- Reread that letter you wrote in step one. Write out your decision to forgive across the bottom. You may want to tear up the letter, nail it to a cross, or burn it as a tangible way to express your decision to trust God in the process of forgiveness.

True forgiveness is one of the most important instructions Jesus gives us. The reality of a fallen world makes forgiveness the only true remedy for the damage done to our souls by hurtful relationships. I challenge you to consider the deep work of forgiveness and let God know that you are willing to practice true forgiveness in your relationship. As you practice true forgiveness, you are well on your way toward ending your cycle of damaging relationships.

Discussion Questions

1. Why does God ask us to forgive?

2. What effect does forgiveness have in our lives?

3. Have you ever experienced forgiveness?

4. What are some of the reasons we don't want to forgive?

5. How is forgiveness possible?

6. Why does God tell us He won't forgive us if we won't forgive others?

CHAPTER SEVEN

What Can Happen When Women Give God Control?

Being out of control is considered a negative condition in our culture. Women have been told that they must take control of their lives. Some people theorize that the reason women don't have more social and economic power in our culture is that they haven't taken enough control. Self-control is the focus of our existence. Those with the most self-control are the ones who make it in the world.

But there is a time when being out of control can be a good thing. When we are experiencing God's control in our lives, everything becomes right with the world. This week we'll consider what it might mean to give God control.

Nancy doesn't consider herself a controlling person. In fact, most often she feels at the mercy of her schedule. She is the mother of three children, each on athletic teams as well as involved in Scouts and children's activities at church. Her husband's job requires that he travel frequently, so Nancy is responsible for arranging rides if any of the children's activities conflict. On top of that, she is a Bible study discussion leader, works in the children's choir, and stuffs the weekly church newsletters. At school she volunteers in the PTA and regularly helps the teachers in any way they will let her. Her weekly calendar is color coded to make sure she doesn't miss a thing.

Deep down, all of this behavior is driven by her controlling personality, resulting in an insatiable pursuit of doing what's right—which means saying yes to every request made of her. She harbors memories of being a regular kid, not having many activities, and always feeling like she missed out on things when she grew up. She never made a conscious choice to make her kids popular or allow them to feel privileged, but that's exactly what she is doing. Her controlling personality is seen in her hypervolunteering, which is based on her shame that she wasn't good enough as a child herself.

After Nancy took the control test, she got mad. She said, "I didn't think I would register as a controlling personality." Her first thought was, *Oh no, now here's another area of my life I'll have to work on.*

Are you like Nancy? Take time to analyze your personal control scale. Let's see if the results surprise you.

Personal Control Scale

How controlling are you? Consider the following questions to evaluate your own control intensity. Place a check by any statements that are true of you.

_____ I know that the best place for my children (or those I love most) is in God's hands.

_____ I am a forgiving person.

_____ People aren't always complaining that I have to be in charge.

_____ My closest friends (or children) do not think I try to run their lives.

_____ It's okay for me not to know what I am going to do tomorrow.
_____ I enjoy unstructured free time at least once a week.
_____ I could honestly tell God that I'm willing to go anywhere to serve Him, if that is His desire.
_____ If I feel the Holy Spirit prodding me to speak to someone about Christ, I do so, even though I might feel embarrassed.
_____ I don't end up doing the majority of work on the committees I serve on.
_____ At least one other person knows the most painful events of my life and has been supportive.
_____ I don't try to look all together on the outside, hiding my real vulnerability.
_____ I don't mind admitting my weaknesses.
_____ Vulnerability isn't a scary condition for me.
_____ I know I'm vulnerable to God, and I wouldn't have it any other way.
_____ I know of at least five areas of my life that all the effort in the world would not give me control over.
_____ I don't feel used by others when I reach out to them and they don't respond.
_____ When working on group projects, I don't feel I have to take over or do everything myself.
_____ When someone tells me a problem, I just listen. I don't feel I have to provide the right answer.
_____ I don't feel overwhelmed with responsibilities.
_____ I rarely have critical thoughts about others.

Total checks __________ x 5 = ____________

Control Scale Results

95–100—Saint. You are so perfectly at peace with God and yourself that you have no control issues. (Or you weren't completely honest with yourself when you took this test.)

85–95—Flexible. You have discovered that control doesn't solve your problems. You yield yourself to God and others.

75–85—Bending. You are aware of a desire for control and battle within yourself between controlling people and situations and yielding them to God.

65–75—Control-Minded. You're caught in a life of control and are in bondage trying to control others.

55–65—Rigid. You have a controlling outlook and find it difficult to see that control is an illusion.

45–55—Controlling Personality. You are deceived by control and are committed to making life work your way.

45 and under—Control Freak. You are living to control people, events, and circumstances and believe control is mandatory for existence.

How did you do? Did you see yourself as a person who needs control before you took the test? Like Nancy, were you surprised by your results? Don't be alarmed! We can't *not* be controlling without God's help. Let's look at why each of us seeks control and how we can let go to find true security in our lives.

Why Do We Control?

Underneath our controlling behavior is our hurt in relationships. We develop our lives of control in order to protect ourselves from more pain and hurt. But I want you to think about this question: "Are you ever really in control?"

> [12]Therefore, my dear friends, as you have always obeyed—
> not only in my presence, but now much more in my
> absence—continue to work out your salvation with fear and
> trembling, [13]for it is God who works in you to will and to
> act according to his good purpose (Philippians 2:12-13).

❧ What is meant here by "work out your salvation"?

❧ Doesn't "working out your salvation" mean that you should be in control?

- What is meant by "it is God who works in you to will and to act according to his good purpose"?

- Could you will to worship God if He weren't working in you?

- Have you ever realized that what you believed were your great ideas or thoughts were given to you by God?

I remember in college having passing thoughts that I would like to write books someday. Now I realize that it was God giving me those thoughts. At the time I didn't think God was involved. I discovered that thinking I am in control of my life is the great delusion I feed myself.

- Make a list of things you think you are in control of. Beside each item on your list, estimate what percentage of control you actually have in that situation. (For example: I can control what I feed my kids, but when they are at friends' houses I don't know what they are eating. Therefore, 90 percent of the time I can control what my children eat.)

Ultimately, we must face the fact that we can control only so much about our lives. And that's the good news. When we realize this fact, we learn to rest in the sovereignty of our God.

> The wise woman builds her house, but with her own hands the foolish one tears hers down (Proverbs 14:1).

Both the wise woman and the foolish woman cause something to happen to their houses. Both use their own hands.

- What happens to their houses?

- Describe how being controlling can hurt relationships.

Control can be an ugly thing. Through pursuing control, we can figuratively "tear down our homes," destroying the relationships within.

❧ How have your efforts to control torn down your house?

It is impossible to fully recover from our need to control (or our need to think we are in control) until we grasp the reality of God's love for us. He asks us to trust Him to be in control, but we would rather control God. The desire to control God is perhaps our greatest spiritual battle. It is most difficult for us to approach God longing for relationship with Him. Most of the time we want Him to show us how to make our lives work better. We follow Him because we want formulas or programs to make our lives and relationships stronger or because we are afraid of what He will do to us if we disobey. God doesn't want that kind of control in our lives. He didn't create us to be robots. He created us with a free will, and nothing pleases Him more than when we freely respond to His love.

God wants us to realize our foolishness in trying to control our world. He isn't pleased when we try to use Him to control our world either. In Revelation 2:1-7, God strongly admonished the church at Ephesus. It was a church that looked great on the outside. The Ephesians were doing everything right—persevering and working hard to keep the Word of God the center of their church. They were not tolerating wicked men and were testing any who claimed to be apostles and were not. They had rigid standards that they had received from God. But God threatened to take their light away because they had left their first love. They were following God out of duty and not in a relationship. That's not good enough for God. He doesn't want dutiful followers. He wants us to follow Him because we love and trust Him. He wants us to obey His commands because we are sure they are right for us.

❧ Have you ever been tempted to follow God out of duty and/or fear?

- How does it make you feel that God is not happy with people who follow Him for those reasons?

- Why do you think God cares so much about whether we love Him or not?

God is the God of letting go. He asks us to let go in many areas of our lives. Read the following Scripture passages and describe what God asks you to let go of and why.

> Cast all your anxiety on him because he cares for you (1 Peter 5:7).

> [28]"Come to me, all you who are weary and burdened, and
> I will give you rest. [29]Take my yoke upon you and learn
> from me, for I am gentle and humble in heart, and you
> will find rest for your souls. [30]For my yoke is easy and my
> burden is light" (Matthew 11:28-30).

> The sacrifices of God are a broken spirit; a broken and contrite heart, O God, you will not despise (Psalm 51:17).

> "Has not my hand made all these things, and so they came into being?" declares the Lord. "This is the one I esteem: he who is humble and contrite in spirit, and trembles at my word" (Isaiah 66:2).

God asks us to let go of anxiety so we can experience His care (1 Peter 5:7). In Matthew 11:28-30 He invites us to let go of our own yokes (the things that drive us) and receive His yoke so that we can find rest for our souls. According to Psalm 51:17, when we let go of our power and become broken and contrite before God, He delights in us. And when we let go of our pride and humble ourselves, we are esteemed by God (Isaiah 66:2).

> [3]We know that we have come to know him if we obey his commands. [4]The man who says, "I know him," but does not do what he commands is a liar, and the truth is not in him. [5]But if anyone obeys his word, God's love is truly made complete in him. This is how we know we are in him: [6]Whoever claims to live in him must walk as Jesus did (1 John 2:3-6).

❧ How do we know that we love God?

Keeping God's commandments is central to love. In fact, you can't keep the spirit and the action of His commands without love. Loving God is a requirement of true obedience.

The world tells us that we need to be in control, but the Bible tells us that we need to give God control. But how do you give God control?

First, you must be His child by trusting in Jesus Christ as the payment for your sin. It is only then that the Holy Spirit comes into your life, enabling you to give God control. Giving Him control begins with surrendering who you are, recognizing that there is nothing you can do or say that makes you or anyone else savable, and receiving God's free gift of salvation.

> Those who obey his commands live in him, and he in them. And this is how we know that he lives in us: We know it by the Spirit he gave us (1 John 3:24).

❧ Describe how the Holy Spirit comes into our lives.

When we obey His command of salvation, the Holy Spirit comes to live in us. We know that Christ lives in us by the presence of the Holy Spirit that we feel in our hearts.

❧ What does the Holy Spirit give us, according to the following passages?

> And hope does not disappoint us, because God has poured out his love into our hearts by the Holy Spirit, whom he has given us (Romans 5:5).

> For the kingdom of God is not a matter of eating and drinking, but of righteousness, peace and joy in the Holy Spirit . . . (Romans 14:17).

> May the God of hope fill you with all joy and peace as you trust in him, so that you may overflow with hope by the power of the Holy Spirit (Romans 15:13).

> [The mystery of Christ] was not made known to men in other generations as it has now been revealed by the Spirit to God's holy apostles and prophets (Ephesians 3:5).

> He saved us, not because of righteous things we had done, but because of his mercy. He saved us through the washing of rebirth and renewal by the Holy Spirit (Titus 3:5).

The Holy Spirit gives us God's love (Romans 5:5). He gives us righteousness, peace and joy (Romans 14:17), and overflowing hope and power (Romans 15:13). The Holy Spirit gives us revelations that prophets of earlier times did not receive (Ephesians 3:5), along with washing, rebirth, and renewal (Titus 3:5).

Women continually tell me that it is hard for them to give their children, careers, spouses, or finances completely to God. They fear that entrusting them to Him would be dangerous. They function with a significant lapse in logic, for what control do we really have in this world, anyway? Control is an illusion we create to make ourselves more comfortable. Though we lack real control, it is still next to impossible for most of us to really give God control.

Steps to Giving God Control of Our Lives

1. Go to God for help. We need to stop looking at ourselves as the resources for our hope, recognizing instead that our help comes from God. We need to let Jesus' example of how to give God control become ours.

> [1]How great is the love the Father has lavished on us, that
> we should be called children of God! And that is what we
> are! The reason the world does not know us is that it did
> not know him. [2]Dear friends, now we are children of
> God, and what we will be has not yet been made known.
> But we know that when he appears, we shall be like him,
> for we shall see him as he is. [3]Everyone who has this hope
> in him purifies himself, just as he is pure (1 John 3:1-3).

❧ How are we made pure?

We are made pure by putting our hope and trust totally in God, His Son, His Word, and the Holy Spirit.

❧ In your journal, write a letter to God asking Him to guide you into the kind of life Jesus lived.

At first, Nancy was angry about the results of her personal control scale. But as she discussed them with the other women in her study group, she realized that the shame she carried from not feeling good enough or special enough as a child was still with her today. In her letter to God she wrote, "Thank You that I don't have to make myself pure by being the volunteer of the month. I'm beginning to see how that just makes me live my life in the opposite way of purity. I end up being consumed by a schedule rather than wallowing in the lavish love You give to me. God, I know I can't be good enough; no one can. I'm not even going to try to stop the craziness through control. I just want to receive Your love for me. I know that You can help me arrange my schedule the right way if I let You. I want to let You. I want to be made pure in Your love, not by my goodness."

2. Admit you are powerless. What power to overcome sin in our lives we miss when we refuse to admit we can't do it on our own! It's like spending the whole afternoon vacuuming the carpet with an unplugged vacuum cleaner. We must plug into the Power Source or we will never overcome our sin. It is our powerlessness that helps us plug into God's powerfulness. We are the plug and He is the outlet.

> But he said to me, "My grace is sufficient for you, for my power is made perfect in weakness." Therefore I will boast all the more gladly about my weaknesses, so that Christ's power may rest on me (2 Corinthians 12:9).

- What happens when we see our weaknesses?

- How can we be safe if we admit we are powerless?

Once you reach the point of admitting you are powerless to make the right choice consistently and productively, you have taken the first step in your healing process. The second step is recognizing Who is powerful!

When will we believe in the power of Jesus? When will we surrender and admit we are powerless? When we do, we will be on our way to giving God control.

3. Let go and let God. What can happen when women give God control? Heaven only knows. That's the beauty of it. When we stop striving, we begin to be still. It is only then that we experience God in a deeper way. We can't get anywhere in our relationship with God until we dump our tendency to control. That's why in Jesus' day, though many religious leaders saw Him face-to-face, they didn't recognize the Person to whom they were speaking. They were too busy trying to control God by their religious endeavors to recognize Him when He stood right in front of them.

> But now he has reconciled you by Christ's physical body through death to present you holy in his sight, without blemish and free from accusation (Colossians 1:22).

- How are you made holy?

- How are you trying to make yourself holy?

- How is God speaking to you today about letting go?

What started out as more discouragement for Nancy (taking the Personal Control Scale) ended up leading her to face the reality of the control she seeks in life and the truth about where real life is found. Through prayer and her new insights, she decided to make some painful decisions. She had each child choose only one sport to participate in. As it turned out, her two daughters chose soccer and her son chose baseball. This left her with the winter season off to regroup and enjoy family time with a less hectic schedule. She stepped down as the Bible study leader and decided she mainly needed a place to come and be supported by other women as just a group member. It was humbling at first, but it was a great decision. She also cut back on her volunteering at school and church.

After a couple of months of letting God be in control, Nancy found herself noticing sunsets and the changing seasons. She started to feel God's love for her in the most unusual moments and smallest ways. She felt a sweet kiss when He favored her with a parking place at a crowded mall. She started to talk to her children more, telling them how much she loved them rather than what they needed to do that day. Nancy began to enjoy being out of control more and more each day.

Sooner or later, if you are going to grow in the Christian life, you are going to have to give God control. And I can guarantee that once you do it, you'll never regret it. If only letting go weren't so hard!

Discussion Questions

1. How does it make you feel that God wants you to give Him control of your life?

2. Can you think of an example of a time that you gave God control of your life? What happened?

3. What do we really have control of in this world, and what *don't* we have control of?

4. Why does God give us a free will?

5. How do you let God control your life?

6. What is your motivation for letting go and letting God?

Chapter Eight

Finding Stillness in a Frantic World

You know, I think I could be a great Christian if . . .

How would you finish that statement?

I think I could be a great Christian if everything went my way; if my husband wouldn't make me mad; if my children would do their homework; if the other drivers weren't so selfish. . . .

Sometimes we feel as if the only way to be great Christians is to escape to the desert and pray all day long. But God says He wants us to be great Christians right now, in the families we live in, in the jobs we love or hate, wherever we are. We become great Christians as we consistently move into God's love, receive His forgiveness and forgive others, and stop trying to be in control. To consistently do this equals Christian growth. So the question becomes, how do we develop consistency in our Christian growth?

The secret to being a great Christian is learning how to rest in God. We've just discovered how to give God control. Deep and lasting spiritual growth is developed through simply being with God. I call this "passive

Christianity." It's not exactly the kind of Christianity we are most comfortable with, so let's go back to Genesis to discover the secret to passivity.

> [2]By the seventh day God had finished the work he had been doing; so on the seventh day he rested from all his work. [3]And God blessed the seventh day and made it holy, because on it he rested from all the work of creating that he had done (Genesis 2:2-3).

- What happens on the seventh day of Creation?
- Why would God rest? Is He tired? Is He lazy?
- Do you think God made a rhythm of rest in His creation? Why or why not?
- How is rest holy?

In my personal life, I have discovered that rest is deeply spiritual. God didn't rest because He was tired or lazy. God created us with a need to set aside time for rest and reflection. When we ignore this important reality, we usually end up burned out and unproductive.

> [11]Make it your ambition to lead a quiet life, to mind your own business and to work with your hands, just as we told you, [12]so that your daily life may win the respect of outsiders and so that you will not be dependent on anybody (1 Thessalonians 4:11-12).

- What are we to make it our ambition to have?

Ambition and a quiet life seem antithetical, don't they? Personally, it has taken a great deal of ambition for me to live a quiet life. I have to work hard to keep my life in balance.

Voices Calling to Us

Because of the way we women are wired, we cannot easily ignore the cries of a child or the needs of an aging mother. We are attuned to the needs of the people around us. Why is it that a son can come home for Christmas and never shed a tear, while a daughter weeps her eyes out? We have a sixth sense about the emotional state of the people around us. Do you hear voices calling you to meet needs? I struggle daily trying to decipher the voices in my head. Can you relate to this example from my journal?

> I feel guilty for the opportunity to be in my pajamas at 9:00 A.M. Although I have much to do and much that could have kept me busy until now, I have chosen to follow Jesus. I have spent my morning preparing to teach my Sunday class about Luke. I probably wouldn't have planned my day this way. I have so many voices offering their "shoulds."
>
> My Brian voice says, "You should be doing. No time for sitting or reflecting: do laundry, scrub floors, teach Benjamin, go to the grocery store, clean, cook, do, do, do."
>
> My Benjamin voice says, "You should be teaching: I should be able to write my name, recognize the alphabet, numbers, shapes, and colors. I should not be watching TV. I should be having friends over to play with. I should not be so strong-willed. All of this is your fault."
>
> My Debi voice says, "You should have the chapters of your book written and sent off; you should do all those things on Brian's list."
>
> Just now I'm not in touch with the voices that demand still more of me: my Rachel voice, church voice, patients' voices, neighborhood voices . . . They can go on and on.

What voices do you hear? Write down the names of the voices in your head and the messages they send you.

Frantic Christianity

The voices we hear and our drive to be everything to everyone spill into our Christian experiences. Women are particularly susceptible to becoming frantic Christians. I often observe a swirl of frantic Christianity among women in the church. There is plenty to do, and we are just the women to do it.

Pamela wants to know God. Her attempts to be close to Him have left her in a tailspin of frantic Christian living. Her pursuits control her money, her time, and her relationships. She has put all her effort into conquering her relationship with God. She supports several different radio ministries. She tithes regularly to her church. She attends every Christian conference that comes to town and buys at least five books that promise to solve her dilemma of not knowing God. She avoids her non-Christian family and tries to make friends with only Christians.

Pamela is trying everything she can to know God and follow Him. Yet each time she helps a new ministry, she feels a greater sense of burnout. She is starting to doubt that it is even possible to know and experience God. What Pamela is experiencing is the very opposite of that. She is making her own way to God, rather than listening to His way for her.

Franticness Comes from the Mirrors We Look Into

What is the source of Pamela's frantic behavior and that of other women like her? Franticness comes from the world's mirrors as they constantly bombard us with ideas about how to better belong here. It comes from the natural instincts of our sinful nature. We strive to be the best, to have it all, to conquer. Without God at the center of our quests, we will find ourselves lost and spinning, chasing the wind and ending up empty.

You won't know God by striving, possessing, or conquering. Romans 11:33 says, "Oh, the depth of the riches of the wisdom and knowledge of God! How unsearchable his judgments, and his paths beyond tracing out!" And in Job 11:7-8 we read, "Can you fathom the mysteries of God? Can you probe the limits of the Almighty? They are higher than the heavens—what can you do? They are deeper than the depths of the grave—what can you know?" There is a depth, a height, an awesome reality, a new frontier to discover. But we'll have to throw away the mirrors we look into and learn instead how to become mirrors ourselves—mirrors that reflect the magnificence of our Creator.

Franticness Comes from Our Need to Be Good Enough

Women are so eager to win approval that we will often go to extremes to make ourselves liked and accepted. We will busy ourselves trying to excel at work and at home. We feel a need to be this way without complaining—and always with a smile.

It was natural for Pamela to think that if she wanted to know God, she needed to give all her money, time, and talent to Him. After all, when she set her mind on being the best advertising executive she could be, that is what was required. Her approach was effective in the workplace, but it resulted in emptiness in her soul.

The opposite of frantic Christianity is passive Christianity. Women are so relationship-centered and sensitive to other people's needs that we won't naturally choose the course of passive Christianity. Yet without learning to listen, to be passive in our relationship with God, we will never get to know Him.

Passive Christianity

Passive Christianity involves being still enough and defenseless enough to look into the mirror of your soul and listen as God speaks to you and is with you. It happens when you set aside your business, your Christian work, and all of your excuses. It means looking at some of the places inside of you that you would rather ignore. Something amazing happens in passive Christianity when we look at our darkest places, because in the light of God's love we are liberated. It is a bittersweet experience, and there is nothing more fulfilling to the soul. Passive Christianity is what Mary experienced and what her sister Martha missed (Luke10:38-42) but later found (John 11, 12).

Frantic Christianity comes naturally to women. Passive Christianity happens through the work of the Holy Spirit in a soul that releases itself to God. This process is deliberate, painful, and amazingly beneficial.

Though it might seem contradictory, finding stillness in a frantic world is a discipline, and discipline requires sacrifice. Let's use commitment to physical exercise as an illustration. For the past five years I've tried to exercise three times a week. Now, there's one thing I want to make you completely aware of: I hate exercise! I'm not one of those marathon runners. I do it as little as I can get by with. Though it is often a struggle to make myself do it, I do it because it is good for me and it keeps me healthy. I've even lowered my cholesterol by exercising regularly. Yet after all this time and the obvious benefits I've witnessed, it still takes discipline for me to exercise.

Spiritual growth is a discipline in much the same way. For example, I discipline myself spiritually by reading my Bible and praying daily. I read Christian books and prepare lessons as a Sunday school teacher. All of this takes discipline. Unlike exercising, most of the time I love to do it. But as with exercise, there are days I do it not because I feel like it but because I know it is good for me. Discipline is hard! Still, it is an important tool for deepening your spiritual life.

Let's take the comparison between exercise and spiritual growth further. Physical exercise requires you to have a healthy heart. It is vital that you consult with your physician before beginning any exercise program. Why? Even though exercise is good for you, there are certain physical conditions that could make exercise bad for you.

Believe it or not, you also need a healthy heart to benefit from spiritual discipline. In fact, you can do damage if you are not spiritually exercising with a healthy heart. In what ways could spiritual exercise cause damage? Let's look at some biblical examples.

Read the following Scripture passages and explain how each person listed acted spiritually on the outside but harbored a weak heart inside. Describe what happened in each case.

Balaam—Numbers 22:7-20

7The elders of Moab and Midian left, taking with them
the fee for divination. When they came to Balaam, they

told him what Balak had said. [8] "Spend the night here," Balaam said to them, "and I will bring you back the answer the Lord gives me." So the Moabite princes stayed with him. [9]God came to Balaam and asked, "Who are these men with you?" [10]Balaam said to God, "Balak son of Zippor, king of Moab, sent me this message: [11]'A people that has come out of Egypt covers the face of the land. Now come and put a curse on them for me. Perhaps then I will be able to fight them and drive them away.' " [12]But God said to Balaam, "Do not go with them. You must not put a curse on those people, because they are blessed." [13]The next morning Balaam got up and said to Balak's princes, "Go back to your own country, for the Lord has refused to let me go with you." [14]So the Moabite princes returned to Balak and said, "Balaam refused to come with us." [15]Then Balak sent other princes, more numerous and more distinguished than the first. [16]They came to Balaam and said: "This is what Balak son of Zippor says: Do not let anything keep you from coming to me, [17]because I will reward you handsomely and do whatever you say. Come and put a curse on these people for me." [18]But Balaam answered them, "Even if Balak gave me his palace filled with silver and gold, I could not do anything great or small to go beyond the command of the Lord my God. [19]Now stay here tonight as the others did, and I will find out what else the Lord will tell me." [20]That night God came to Balaam and said, "Since these men have come to summon you, go with them, but do only what I tell you."

Ananias and Sapphira—Acts 5:1-11

[1]Now a man named Ananias, together with his wife Sapphira, also sold a piece of property. [2]With his wife's full knowledge he kept back part of the money for himself, but brought the rest and put it at the apostles' feet. [3]

Then Peter said, "Ananias, how is it that Satan has so filled your heart that you have lied to the Holy Spirit and have kept for yourself some of the money you received for the land? [4]Didn't it belong to you before it was sold? And after it was sold, wasn't the money at your disposal? What made you think of doing such a thing? You have not lied to men but to God." [5]When Ananias heard this, he fell down and died. And great fear seized all who heard what had happened. [6]Then the young men came forward, wrapped up his body, and carried him out and buried him. [7]About three hours later his wife came in, not knowing what had happened. [8]Peter asked her, "Tell me, is this the price you and Ananias got for the land?" "Yes," she said, "that is the price." [9]Peter said to her, "How could you agree to test the Spirit of the Lord? Look! The feet of the men who buried your husband are at the door, and they will carry you out also." [10]At that moment she fell down at his feet and died. Then the young men came in and, finding her dead, carried her out and buried her beside her husband. [11]Great fear seized the whole church and all who heard about these events.

The Pharisees—Mark 12:38-40

[38]As he taught, Jesus said, "Watch out for the teachers of the law. They like to walk around in flowing robes and be greeted in the marketplaces, [39]and have the most important seats in the synagogues and the places of honor at banquets. [40]They devour widows' houses and for a show make lengthy prayers. Such men will be punished most severely."

Judas—John 12:1-6

[1]Six days before the Passover, Jesus arrived at Bethany, where Lazarus lived, whom Jesus had raised from the dead. [2]Here a

> dinner was given in Jesus' honor. Martha served, while
> Lazarus was among those reclining at the table with him.
> [3]Then Mary took about a pint of pure nard, an expensive
> perfume; she poured it on Jesus' feet and wiped his feet with
> her hair. And the house was filled with the fragrance of the
> perfume. [4]But one of his disciples, Judas Iscariot, who was
> later to betray him, objected, [5]"Why wasn't this perfume sold
> and the money given to the poor? It was worth a year's
> wages." [6]He did not say this because he cared about the poor
> but because he was a thief; as keeper of the money bag, he
> used to help himself to what was put into it.

Balaam didn't care about God's people. He was motivated by the material gain he could receive from Israel's enemies. Ananias and Sapphira gave money to the church but lied. The Pharisees took on leadership roles in the church so that they could be honored by men. Judas portrayed concern for the poor but really stole from the proceeds given on behalf of the poor.

You can avoid "heart failure" by taking the following five steps toward spiritual exercise, which parallel principles of effective physical exercise.

Five Steps Toward Spiritual Discipline

1. Listen to the voice of the instructor. When you are doing physical exercise, it is important to listen to your instructor. She will tell you if your body is out of line and show you how to get the most out of each exercise. I think the reason that a lot of women don't feel close to God, and in fact feel alienated from Him, is because they don't know His voice. Too many Christian women hear God as some pastor's voice telling them to spend 30 minutes a day with Him or they will fail as Christians. They hear their Bible study leader's voice telling them that if they would just live the way she does, all would be well. They hear their mother's voice saying they'd better do better or God won't like them. Most of these people don't mean to communicate defeating and hurtful messages. And often women project these voices onto others. They don't consider that God would want to talk to them personally. But He does.

> "When he has brought out all his own, he goes on ahead of them, and his sheep follow him because they know his voice" (John 10:4).

- Who knows Jesus' voice?

Jesus' sheep know His voice and follow that voice.

- Revelation 12:10 says that Satan is the accuser of the brethren. Give an example of the kind of statements Satan may make about you. (Examples: My kids are a mess, so I have been a terrible mother. I shouldn't have a fat little tummy; I have no self-discipline.)

- In your journal write down the voices that tell you who you are and what you should be doing. List 10 statements that are in your head right now.

- Read over these statements and check those that come from God. Cross out the others. Be discerning of the voices in your head that tell you what you need to be.

2. Endure when you see little benefit. If you expect to see immediate results from your new workout program, you are going to be disappointed. It would be foolish to give up exercising because after one day your flab hasn't gone away or you don't have the extra energy you expected. The benefits of physical exercise come only with time and consistency. Results will come if you remain committed. It's the same with spiritual discipline. You may still yell at your children or be impatient with other drivers or gossip at the watercooler, but please don't give up! Even the great saints of the Bible struggled with this. Read the words of Paul in Philippians 3:12.

> Not that I have already obtained all this, or have already been made perfect, but I press on to take hold of that for which Christ Jesus took hold of me.

❧ What is Paul's attitude about spiritual growth?

Paul recognized that he hadn't already attained spiritual perfection, but that didn't stop him from pressing forward.

> Now faith is being sure of what we hope for and certain of what we do not see (Hebrews 11:1).

❧ How does not seeing results affect spiritual growth?

A great spiritual writer from the seventeenth century, Jeanne Guyon, promises that God will bring clouds that block our full view of Him to build our faith. "And yet it is true that this God who desires to give Himself to you will often conceal Himself from you—from you, the very one who seeks Him! . . . Now why would God do that? Dear saint of God, you must learn the ways of your Lord. Yours is a God who often hides Himself for a purpose. Why? His purpose is to rouse you from spiritual laziness. His purpose in removing Himself from you is to cause you to pursue Him."[3]

3. Celebrate the changes you do recognize. I already mentioned the lowering of my cholesterol after I had been exercising six months; it went down even more after 18 months. I also find that my muscles can do more for me since I began exercising. My arms and legs are stronger. I feel healthier. I like the way exercise affects my overall outlook on life and my body. Even though I still hate to exercise, all of this motivates me to keep at it. It's the same spiritually. As we celebrate what God has done in our lives, we'll find motivation to seek Him and love Him more. Focus on the strides you are making, no matter how small they may seem.

Read on in Philippians 3:13-14.

> [13]Brothers, I do not consider myself yet to have taken hold of it. But one thing I do: Forgetting what is behind and straining toward what is ahead, [14]I press on toward the goal to win the prize for which God has called me heavenward in Christ Jesus.

- Are you living up to what you have already obtained?

- How is your life different since you became a Christian?

- How are you more like Christ in this last year?

Once I was so overwhelmed with the trials in my life that I decided to have a talk with God. I poured myself a cup of tea, sat down at the kitchen table, and addressed God as if He were my best friend sitting there beside me. I can't remember any particular thought He gave me or much about our interaction that day, but I do remember the days that followed. Brian asked me what was different about me. My immediate reaction was, "I don't know." I couldn't think of anything that had changed. Then I remembered my teatime with God and realized that the experience had done something deep in my soul that I hadn't even recognized. I've had many similar encounters with God since then.

> ...Being confident of this, that he who began a good work in you will carry it on to completion until the day of Christ Jesus (Philippians 1:6).

- Describe how Paul saw the Philippians spiritually.

Would Paul be able to say these same words about you?

Paul was able to identify evidence of spiritual growth in the lives of the people in Philippi. He was confident that since the Spirit was working in their lives, He would continue to do so.

4. Make spiritual goals for yourself. After you begin an exercise program, you need to increase the weights you are lifting or the distance you are running or the speed at which you run if you are to get the best outcome from your program. You don't want your spiritual life to stay just where it was last year. God is ever calling us to deeper and deeper commitment to Him. This deeper and deeper commitment brings deeper and deeper joy in our lives. We need to make goals for ourselves.

When I first started my exercise program, I exercised for 15 minutes. I slowly increased the kind of exercises I did and the length of time I committed to exercise. Now I exercise about 45 to 60 minutes. It is important to do that with your spiritual goals as well. If you are a mom with young children at home, it may take a lot to find five minutes that you can spend with God. Make that your goal and don't feel guilty that you can't do more at this time. For example, take the first five minutes that your children are down for a nap to sit down and talk to God and read one verse from the Bible. Remember, reaching spiritual goals doesn't depend on the time you spend; it depends on the desire you have to hear from God and connect with Him. He can show you how to feel close to Him while you are doing the laundry or cleaning the house.

Maybe time isn't your problem. Perhaps you are newly retired and suddenly bombarded with time but don't naturally feel like spending it listening to God. I suggest you make a spiritual goal of watching for God during this transition of life. Ask Him to show you new friends and new ways that you can enjoy your relationship with Him. Go out for a walk around your neighborhood and ask God to bless each house that you pass. The key is to start out slowly and take into account your stage of life, whatever it might be. Give yourself permission to take small steps.

❧ What spiritual goals have you set for yourself?

5. Schedule time for rest and recovery. Physical exercise is draining. During a workout it is important to schedule a cool-down time. We observed at the beginning of this chapter that God created this world with a rhythm of rest. Jesus demonstrated that need for rest. So many of His miracles were performed on the Sabbath to teach that He was the God of the Sabbath and that miracles performed in God's name are not energy-drainers.

We have a culture that doesn't respect the need for rest, so people are driven to perform and achieve and accomplish. We think we will miss out on something important if we stop to rest. The truth is that we will miss out on something important if we don't schedule rest into our lives.

> Jesus went out as usual to the Mount of Olives, and his disciples followed him (Luke 22:39).

This verse marks the beginning of that great event that we ponder every Easter season, Jesus' prayer in the garden.

❧ How did Judas know that they could find Jesus there?

Jesus went, as was usual for Him, to the Mount of Olives to pray. This was the rhythm and pattern of His life. That is why Judas knew where to find Him.

If you take the time to read through the gospels, you will notice something about Jesus. He took time to rest and time to be with God alone in prayer. He loved to pray in places like this. He longed to enjoy rest and fellowship with God in the garden.

Here's a challenge for you this week. I encourage you to go to a park or garden for 30 minutes to spend time alone with God. Take along your Bible and a journal to record your thoughts, but nothing else. Find a quiet place and ask God to show you how to rest in Him. Jeanne Guyon has some suggestions, such as slowly repeating, phrase by phrase, a familiar Bible passage and being quiet as you let God speak to you and visualize each phrase. For example, you could use the Lord's Prayer. You would say "Our Father." Then you would pause and visualize that reality. You are praying to your Father; feel the intimacy of that. Grasp the force of those words. Don't move forward until you have finished receiving everything God wants to give you from that phrase. Then move to "Who art in heaven." Picture God in heaven. . . .

- Record the memories of your garden time with God in your journal.
- What did you experience?
- What did you learn about God?
- What did you learn about yourself?
- Would you want to do this again? If so, how often. Make a goal!

Spiritual Disciplines

Here are some spiritual disciplines you can practice to exercise your soul. (You can learn more about these disciplines in Richard Foster's book *Celebration of Discipline.*)

Inward Disciplines

Meditation—This involves memorizing and reflecting on short passages of Scripture and asking God what He has to tell you through them. The more I have meditated on Genesis 1–3, the basis of this book, the more insights I have received. I've memorized most of the passages, without specifically deciding to do that. It's as if these passages have become a part of me, they are so deeply ingrained in my brain.

Prayer—Prayer is a two-way communication with God. It involves listening, attentiveness, and communion. It is actually enjoying the privilege of God's presence. Sometimes it goes beyond human words and thoughts (Romans 8:26-27). We can pray anytime, anywhere, about anything. Prayer is not about poetic words that turn the heart of heaven in our direction; rather, prayer reflects the cry of a sincere and contrite heart.

Fasting—In my own life, I have practiced fasting when I had to make important decisions and wanted to be sure I heard God's voice. A fast doesn't have to mean abstinence from food. You can abstain from watching TV, for example. Whatever you abstain from, the purpose of fasting is to tune in to God and His love and to invite Him more deeply into your life.

Study—Studying the Bible is different from meditating upon it. When you meditate upon the Bible, you are seeking to understand what God may be saying to you personally. When you study the Bible, you are more focused on understanding what God is saying to everyone. You examine the context of the passage; you consult with the scholars. You seek to understand as best you can the original intention of the passage. I really appreciate the efforts of Precept Ministries, Bible Study Fellowship, and others in their disciplined efforts to help women study the Word of God. Of course, in study we do see our own lives, and God speaks to us there. However, the intention of the discipline is to correctly handle the Word of truth as instructed in 2 Timothy 2:15.

Outward Disciplines

Simplicity—This is a spiritual discipline we women could practice more. If we looked in our closets right now, how many pairs of shoes would we find? What about outfits? How may extra "toys," such as stereos, TV sets, and cars, do we have that we could easily do without? We can simplify our eating habits. God might lead you to eat out less and save that money to share with a food pantry. Invite God to lead you down the path of simplicity. Don't do it by your own effort. God leads us to the discipline of simplicity when we recognize that all of our material possessions can't compare to a relationship with Him.

Solitude—This may be a scary word to some readers. Women define themselves so tightly by their relationships that some may fear being alone. Solitude is the complete opposite of loneliness. Loneliness can exist in the middle of a crowd. For solitude, it is necessary to be away from eye contact and conversation with other human beings. It is the discipline of being with God. It has no agenda. It is listening and abiding with the One who loves us. It is during these periods of solitude that we are changed in our countenances, our values, our beliefs, and our endurance. It isn't a change of our own making. Our part is to choose to spend this time with God. I enjoy times of solitude as I take a nature walk. Sometimes I bring along my Bible or another book that leads me on a reflective exercise. Sometimes I look up at the clouds and simply wonder at the beauty of my Creator.

Submission—Here's another unpopular word! Submission is the discipline of letting go. It is giving God control of our lives and willingly obeying whatever He calls us to do, whether that means keeping our mouths shut when we think we have the answer or forgiving someone who has hurt us deeply. Obedience's outward action will differ for each circumstance and situation. But it has the same internal motivator: a mustard seed of faith in the God who calls us to it.

Service—When service is a spiritual discipline, there is nothing so rewarding to a heart. We won't need to be recognized. In fact, we will yearn to be anonymous because our service becomes a privileged opportunity to participate with God in His work. It won't be our idea, our effort, or our gifts. It will be our moment to lay another crown before our deserving King. We serve God because we love Him, and we realize that serving Him is a privilege. We are not trying to settle our debt to Him through serving Him, because Christ has paid off that debt completely. Rather, service to God is simply the response of a grateful heart.

Corporate Disciplines

Confession—Here's a spiritual discipline that we don't often see practiced in daily life or corporate worship in many churches. There is a beautiful spirit that accompanies a meeting of believers who join in support of one another as they practice public confession. On the rare occasions I have experienced this discipline in the body of Christ, judgments and gossip were stifled by the beauty of sinners admitting their needs. No one feels immune from sin when confronted by Jesus' words in John 8:7: "If any one of you is without sin, let him be the first to throw a stone at her."

Worship—How grateful I am to the hymn writers who speak words of worship that I'm not sure I would utter on my own. "Crown Him with Many Crowns" and "Holy, Holy, Holy" are two of the hymns that help me picture God as I worship. There is nothing like worship with other believers as we experience His presence in our midst.

Guidance—As we look into God's Word together, we receive guidance and instruction for our lives. We learn from the Word and from one another what God has to teach us. We receive guidance from pastors, friends, and mentors. We need direction for our lives from godly people. When the Word of God is offered in corporate worship, it changes our lives. It is an opportunity to praise and worship God, who communes with us through His Word.

Celebration—Celebrating the joy of knowing God with other believers stimulates our souls and prepares us for the joy of heaven. We can worship and praise God in the privacy of our own homes, but it hardly compares with corporate celebration.

Other Disciplines

Another avenue of spiritual growth is reading spiritual books. I have found deep comfort and even a sort of friendship with men and women who lived hundreds of years ago. Words they left behind have led me to a deeper relationship with Jesus. I think every Christian should read *The Pursuit of God* by A. W. Tozer. Another important Christian classic is *The Imitation of Christ* by Thomas à Kempis.

We can also find peace by going on spiritual retreats, finding someone to be our spiritual director, and asking someone to disciple us.

Something I have found helpful in addressing franticness is to take Sundays off. When I choose not to catch up on work and chores on Sundays, I enjoy my week much more.

Keeping a prayer journal has been an important method of spiritual growth for me. I am often amazed at how my journal entries minister to me as I reread them.

> ❧ In your journal, list some spiritual disciplines you can practice to help you grow spiritually.

We will be constantly tempted toward franticness and away from God. When I read about the temptation of Christ (Luke 4:1-13), I think, *What a proud moment that was for God the Father! Here was His Son being tempted in all the ways that we are, and that Adam and Eve were, yet trusting so completely in the character of the Father that He stopped Satan in his tracks.*

On days I'm disgusted with myself for really blowing it, I'm tempted to listen to that voice that tells me to give up. Then I admit, "God, I've really blown it now. I need You more than ever." There's nothing that pleases Him more. He doesn't want me to try to be the best person in the world in my own strength. He longs for me to realize my limitations and come to Him just as I am. When I admit my weakness and brokenness, only then am I truly strong, just as Paul said (2 Corinthians 12:10).

Discussion Questions

1. What evidence of spiritual development have you seen in yourself since you became a Christian?
2. How do we grow as Christians?
3. Why don't we see immediate results from our efforts?
4. How do we keep our goals and priorities for spiritual growth?
5. Do you see the rhythm of rest that God planned in creation as being applicable to us today? Why or why not?
6. How do we listen to God's voice?

Chapter Nine

Understanding Men

We wouldn't even try to tackle this subject without going right back to Genesis to get the scoop. Whether married or not, we all have the privilege of living and ministering in this world with men. That's the way God set it up. We've spent a great deal of time understanding how special we women are to God. Well, men are equally unique and special to Him. I don't think we can fully appreciate our feminine identity unless we equally esteem how special men are. I also think that if we will let men be men and women be women, we will overcome many barriers that keep us apart. It helps us let go of the unimportant things and focus on the right things in life.

In college, Regina found that the answer to the problem of men was to become a feminist and proclaim herself equal to them in every way. She totally ignored the physical and psychological characteristics that were so obvious. That kind of thinking just built walls between her and the men in her life. Claiming equality while denying the differences didn't develop close and satisfying relationships with men. In college, she seemed stuck, always trying to prove something that just didn't exist in her relationships with men. Men and women are different. It requires acknowledgment of that fact if we are to build strong relationships.

Let's review Genesis 2:5-25, this time focusing on what we can learn about men. (See chapter three for these scriptures.)

- How did God create a man? (Genesis 2:7)

- What was the first mention of the man in the context of? (Genesis 2:5)

- Describe the man's existence in the garden before Eve. (Genesis 2:7-17)

- How did the man feel about Eve? (Genesis 2:23)

- How were the man and woman equal? What tasks or responsibilities did they share according to Genesis 1:27-31? According to Genesis 2:24-25? According to Genesis 3:7?

- In Genesis 3:1-6, how were the man and woman tempted differently?

Also note 1 Timothy 2:14, "And Adam was not the one deceived; it was the woman who was deceived and became a sinner."

- While women's pain stems from their relationships, where does the greatest pain for a man come from, as found in Genesis 3:17-19?

Man was created from the dust of the ground. He came into being when God breathed into his nostrils (Genesis 2:7). The first mention of a man in Genesis 2:5 is in the context of performing a task, specifically cultivating plants. Before Eve was created, Adam enjoyed his life in the garden and his relationship with God (Genesis 2:7-17). It was God who recognized that Adam needed Eve. When Adam first laid eyes on Eve, he immediately connected to her and was pleased by their new relationship (Genesis 2:23). Both man and woman were created in the image of God and were charged with ruling the animals and creation (Genesis 1:27-31). Both were naked and unashamed (Genesis 2:24-25). Both were fully accountable to God for their sin (Genesis 3:7). There are differences in the way they were tempted. Eve was deceived by the serpent. Adam was not deceived; he understood fully that he was disobeying God when he ate (Genesis 3:1-6; 1 Timothy 2:14). Man's greatest pain, according to Genesis 3:17-19, will be found in his inability to make things work. He will have thorns and thistles to deal with as he tries to carve out a life for himself and those he loves.

> ❧ In earlier chapters we looked at how women try to control their relationships so they can control their pain. From what you've seen about men, what do you think they would try to control?

When men aren't able to make life work right, as they struggle with the thorns and thistles of life, they react by either getting angry and blaming someone for the problem or by withdrawing and avoiding the problem.

John was a big-time blamer. He grew up in a physically abusive home, where his dad took out his rage on John regularly. John did cause a lot of problems that should have prompted fair parental discipline, but what he got was violence and rage from an angry dad. John carried that pattern into his marriage to Jennifer. When things weren't going well at John's workplace, Jennifer could do one thing that set him off, and he would beat her up. This pattern of domestic violence took a firm hold on both of their lives until Jennifer took a stand and fled to a women's shelter. Jennifer loved John, but she realized that she wasn't the problem. She wasn't the one who made John act out in violence. She realized John had a pattern of behavior that only John could stop. She also discovered that she had become a part of that pattern by believing she caused his violence when she made what John called "stupid decisions."

Other men try to control their pain through withdrawal. We even witnessed Adam withdrawing in the garden as he watched Eve take the bite of fruit without warning or instructing her against it.

Glenda seemed to attract withdrawing men. She had developed a pattern of dating men who wouldn't commit to her. She was always understanding and patient, but after the third serious relationship in a row ended in a slow, painful breakup due to his unwillingness to commit, she decided to try to get smarter about men. She finally realized she was trying to find men she could rescue. Once she felt more secure in her true identity as God's daughter, she felt safe to date a man who was a little more threatening but a lot more healthy.

A big mistake a lot of women make in their relationships with men is they expect men to think like women. The more we discover about gender differences in brains, the more we realize the significance of how the Bible recognizes the differences between men and women.

Men and Women Are Different

Men and women apply different perspectives to problems. When both male and female perspectives are respected and considered, generally good decisions result. Whether the decisions are made by married partners, church committees, or business executives, male and female perspectives together expose dimensions neither sees alone.

To guide us to a better understanding of men, I want to highlight four major areas where men's and women's perspectives differ.

1. A man's greatest fear is failure. From boyhood, a man is conditioned to avoid failure. Just as a girl's greatest pain is centered in her relationships, a boy's greatest pain is centered in his inadequacies. As we've already noted, a woman defines herself by her relationships, and a man defines himself by his accomplishments. He fears failure in sports, school, and other undertakings. He is conditioned to believe that he is supposed to be strong, always have the answers, be independent, and know his way without asking for help. Well, we women know very well that all men fail us. We can do much to help them understand and grow from their failures if we break away from the pressures we put on them not to fail us.

How do you see the men in your life trying to avoid failure?

2. Men are more aggressive than women. Hormones affect men and women differently. Men and women both produce testosterone and estrogen. The amount and proportions vary greatly. Men produce some estrogen, but it occurs in much higher amounts in women. In women, estrogen fluctuates with the monthly cycle—in fact, it helps control the cycle—and contributes to mood swings. In turn, women produce some testosterone, but it is primarily a male hormone and is found in higher amounts in men. Testosterone affects aggression. Basically, the man is chemically better suited to act in aggressive and angry ways. Part of his conditioning against admitting failure will lead him to believe that tears, hurt, or fear are weaknesses that might produce or magnify failure.

Women have a useful opportunity here to call men to account about their aggressiveness. In this way, we call them to greatness. A truly successful man learns how to control and manage his natural tendencies toward aggression rather than allowing them to hurt himself and others.

It is mandatory that women maintain appropriate boundaries when it comes to men's aggressive behaviors. A woman is not responsible for the way a man manages his anger, but she is responsible for how she receives the anger. She should not allow his anger to be detrimental to their relationship. She needs to hold him accountable for dealing with this God-given aspect of his personality.

The fear of failure (or loss of face, which is failure of a sort) is a major factor in influencing a man's aggression as well. When he feels shame or inadequacy, he might try to overpower these negative emotions with aggression and anger. Generally, he is more comfortable with aggression than he is with shame.

❧ Do you respond appropriately to aggression from men in your world?

3. Men are generally more logical than women. Men's left-brain, straight-line logic often gives them an unemotional perspective on situations. Much of the marriage counseling that I do focuses on helping wives recognize that their husbands don't think the same way they do. Women expect men to have the same emotional makeup as women, or at least an emotional makeup that women can understand.

It's important for women to respect this part of men (even though it drives us crazy at times). When a woman is willing to see the logical perspective, she might be better able to invite a man to listen to the emotional perspective. Men are emotional beings, but they need time, patience, and help in identifying and expressing their emotions.

❧ What do you appreciate most about the logical nature of men?

4. Men are sexual beings. My husband says that the way sex influences a man's behavior and thinking is difficult for a woman to relate to or fully understand. Men are conditioned to believe that manhood is sexuality, and they see themselves as powerful when they are sexual. This can be threatening, frightening, and frustrating for women. A woman can accept that a man is different from her and do what she can in the way she dresses and interacts with him to make his battle less difficult. A woman must not take responsibility for a man's sexual struggles; only he can overcome his temptations through Christ. Women can be sensitive to this struggle in men without taking responsibility for it.

❧ Read the following passages and notice the different instructions to husbands and wives.

> 18Wives, submit to your husbands, as is fitting in the
> Lord. 19Husbands, love your wives and do not be harsh
> with them (Colossians 3:18-19).

[21]Submit to one another out of reverence for Christ. [22]Wives, submit to your husbands as to the Lord. [23]For the husband is the head of the wife as Christ is the head of the church, his body, of which he is the Savior. [24]Now as the church submits to Christ, so also wives should submit to their husbands in everything. [25]Husbands, love your wives, just as Christ loved the church and gave himself up for her [26]to make her holy, cleansing her by the washing with water through the word, [27]and to present her to himself as a radiant church, without stain or wrinkle or any other blemish, but holy and blameless. [28]In this same way, husbands ought to love their wives as their own bodies. He who loves his wife loves himself. [29]After all, no one ever hated his own body, but he feeds and cares for it, just as Christ does the church—[30]for we are members of his body. [31]"For this reason a man will leave his father and mother and be united to his wife, and the two will become one flesh." [32]This is a profound mystery—but I am talking about Christ and the church. [33]However, each one of you also must love his wife as he loves himself, and the wife must respect her husband (Ephesians 5:21-33).

[1]Wives, in the same way be submissive to your husbands so that, if any of them do not believe the word, they may be won over without words by the behavior of their wives, [2]when they see the purity and reverence of your lives. [3]Your beauty should not come from outward adornment, such as braided hair and the wearing of gold jewelry and fine clothes. [4]Instead, it should be that of your inner self, the unfading beauty of a gentle and quiet spirit, which is of great worth in God's sight. [5]For this is the way the holy women of the past who put their hope in God used to make themselves beautiful. They were submissive to their own husbands, [6]like Sarah, who obeyed Abraham and

> called him her master. You are her daughters if you do what is right and do not give way to fear. [7]Husbands, in the same way be considerate as you live with your wives, and treat them with respect as the weaker partner and as heirs with you of the gracious gift of life, so that nothing will hinder your prayers (1 Peter 3:1-7).

- In your journal, record how God gives different instructions to men and women.

In Colossians, husbands are told to love their wives and not be harsh with them, and wives are told to submit to their husbands. Ephesians instructs husbands: Love your wife as you love yourself, the way Christ loves the church. Wives are told to submit to and respect their husbands. First Peter tells husbands to be considerate of their wives and treat them with respect, and directs wives to submit and win their husbands with their behavior and attitudes.

Each of these instructions makes perfect sense when you accept that God created us to be different. The woman's instructions lead her to minister to the deepest longing of her husband's heart—to be respected. Likewise, the instructions to the man lead him to give a woman what she most wants in life—his love and relationship.

- Did you learn something new or were you surprised by anything you learned?

- In light of these biblical differences, how do you feel about yourself as a woman? Do you feel God's love and care for you?

- What did you learn about men that applies to the man/men in your life?

- What would you say are a man's greatest needs from the women in his life?

Calling Men to Greatness

Some people might argue that men are the way they are by nature. Since their hormones and brain function make them more fearful of failure, more aggressive, more sexual, and more logical, why not let them be the way they were created to be? John Trent and Gary Smalley have a good answer to that question. "As believers, we never were called to be 'natural' men but spiritual men—men of God who have a lower (human) nature but a higher calling."[4]

As women we have a unique opportunity to call the men in our lives to greatness. We do this as our nature exposes how men's natural way of being is not healthy and needs the Holy Spirit's power to transform them for intimate relationships. In our accepting presence, our men can learn to risk failure. They will find that they need to go deeper emotionally, beyond their natural anger and aggression, to meet us emotionally and find unity. They will also perceive that having great sex involves nurturing and pleasing their wives, not just satisfying themselves. They will discover that their logical thinking is valuable but also limiting at times, especially when figuring out relationships. Our relationships with men call them to greatness. We invite them to become the men God means for them to be.

What Is Your Ministry in a Man's Life?

I know this study is just a beginning, but it should give you a jump start on understanding a man from God's perspective. I can't encourage you enough to understand that men are different from women, that God made it that way, that God loves men and women equally, and that both are special to Him.

Discussion Questions

1. What is the best way to understand a man?

2. What is a man's greatest pain?

3. How do women affect how men see themselves?

4. What is great about men?

5. How does God use men?

6. How can you encourage a man?

Chapter Ten

Liking the Body You Live In

Sit down with a group of women for more than 30 minutes, and sooner or later one of them will begin to talk about her body. It can crop up during the fellowship time at the women's Bible study, while piling it on at the salad bar, during coffee breaks, or while comparing thigh diameters with your best friend over the phone. You can bet that a woman's opinion of her body will not be complimentary. Women are notorious for hating their bodies.

Women's body-image issues have been getting more severe in recent years. Cindi is one example of the girls that come through my counseling office each year. She's 16 years old, above average in appearance, and totally in despair about how she looks. She believes she is ugly because her thighs meet when she stands straight. The past summer at cheerleading camp, one of the girls mentioned that her standard about whether she was thin enough was if there was light between her thighs when she stood straight. Cindi has very muscular legs. They give her outstanding leverage for her jumps and stunts, but they do meet when she stands with her legs straight. She liked her legs until that week. Now, she's throwing up to rid herself of her monstrous thighs.

What is body image, what does it have to do with sexuality, and how do these fleshly, worldly issues tie in with God and how He made us?

Good questions. These may not be our most pressing questions each day, but they are important because the answers can erode our self-confidence, especially beneath the conscious level. Most women fall short of full-fledged body hatred. But many aren't as fortunate and end up suffering from obsessions with their looks, anorexia nervosa, bulimia, repetitive cosmetic surgery, or chronic dieting. And is there a woman among us who hasn't sold unused exercise equipment at a garage sale?

A sign that you are becoming the confident woman God created you to be is that you are free to accept your body, even though you know its flaws. Our culture is unquestionably obsessed with bodies and sexuality. Men and women are constantly being pressured to pursue a certain body type. A woman who keeps her body in perspective understands that her earthly body is simply the garage for her soul while she lives here on earth. A confident woman has a healthy body image.

I once worked with a woman who had lost a lot of weight. She would still be considered heavy by our society's standards, but she was proud of having lost weight. She was excited that she could now fit into the fashions for larger women. She had a remarkable talent for coordinating outfits and truly enjoyed it. She also enjoyed her healthier body. No one was beating down her door asking her to do a fashion magazine cover, but you would have thought so from the way she saw herself. She finally felt beautiful. Her new clothes made the most of her appearance, and the weight loss was a catalyst to maintain her new look. At the same time she was shedding weight, she was growing closer to God. More important than what was happening to her on the outside was what was going on inside—something so deep and compelling that it overcame any negative messages from the world.

This woman had an anchor for her soul. She knew her body was much healthier and that she had achieved a great deal. She was going to be the best woman in the body she had. So if people sneered at her in a bathing suit, they'd better watch out, because she was likely to give them a response that would blow them away.

❧ Think a minute. What was the last thought you had about your body?

Was it after you got out of the shower and caught a glance of your round tummy? Was it while you were putting your lipstick on and you noticed your new wrinkles? You don't have to write it down, but think about it. Was it a positive thought? Most of us think about our bodies in negative ways far too much!

❧ How should we think about our bodies?

❧ How does God want you to feel about your body?

What is a healthy body image? A healthy body image combines acceptance of and respect for the body you have been given.

❧ Who chose the color of your hair and your eyes, your height? Do you trust His choices for you?

> Who of you by worrying can add a single hour to his life? (Matthew 6:27)

❧ Write down the question Jesus asked and the answer to that question.

Well, who can add a centimeter to her height by worrying? The answer is obvious, isn't it?

We are not the only generation obsessed and worried about our bodies and what we put on them.

❧ Read the message Jesus gave to His followers in Luke 12:22-31.

> 22Then Jesus said to his disciples: "Therefore I tell you, do
> not worry about your life, what you will eat; or about
> your body, what you will wear. 23Life is more than food,
> and the body more than clothes. 24Consider the ravens:
> They do not sow or reap, they have no storeroom or barn;
> yet God feeds them. And how much more valuable you
> are than birds! 25Who of you by worrying can add a single
> hour to his life? 26Since you cannot do this very little
> thing, why do you worry about the rest? 27Consider how
> the lilies grow. They do not labor or spin. Yet I tell you,
> not even Solomon in all his splendor was dressed like one
> of these. 28If that is how God clothes the grass of the field,
> which is here today, and tomorrow is thrown into the fire,
> how much more will he clothe you, O you of little faith!
> 29And do not set your heart on what you will eat or drink;
> do not worry about it. 30For the pagan world runs after all
> such things, and your Father knows that you need them.
> 31But seek his kingdom, and these things will be given to
> you as well.

❧ Why does Jesus tell us not to worry about our bodies?

❧ Who runs after what she will eat or drink?

❧ How will these things be taken care of if we don't worry about them?

People without belief in God (called pagans) worry about their bodies and their bodily needs. But Jesus tells us not to worry about our bodily needs or appearance, because if we believe Him and take Him at His word, He promises that He will take care of all that we need.

Jesus Had a Body

If Jesus hadn't had a body, He couldn't have shed His blood and given His body as our perfect sacrifice. Our own bodies have a similar importance. In our bodies we glorify God and minister with the hands and feet and eyes that He gave us.

❧ What does Isaiah 53:2 tell us about Jesus' appearance?

> He grew up before him like a tender shoot, and like a root out of dry ground. He had no beauty or majesty to attract us to him, nothing in his appearance that we should desire him.

We don't know what Jesus looked like. We do know that He didn't have any physical characteristics that would draw people to Him.

❧ According to Luke 2:52, what do you know about Jesus' physical development?

> And Jesus grew in wisdom and stature, and in favor with God and men.

When it says that Jesus grew in stature, it is referring to the natural process of development that human bodies go through. Jesus went through the changes of adolescence, all the way to some of the adjustments of adulthood (He may have had a gray hair or two in His head before He died.)

> [15]And he said to them, "I have eagerly desired to eat this Passover with you before I suffer. [16]For I tell you, I will not eat it again until it finds fulfillment in the kingdom of God" (Luke 22:15-16).

❧ How does the act of Communion relate to Jesus' body and how He used it?

The main reason that God sent Jesus to us in human flesh was because He required a sacrifice for sin. Communion reminds us that Jesus' body was the sacrifice necessary for us to be reconciled to God.

Jesus is the perfect example for us women of how to focus on our bodies. Jesus accepted His body and didn't argue with God about how He was made. He knew that God specifically chose not to give Him physical characteristics that would attract people. God wanted men and women who were moved by the Spirit to be drawn to Him.

- Have you ever felt drawn to a spiritual person who doesn't have the physical characteristics that are valued in our culture?

- What drew you to that person?

- Do you think God put thought into that person's physical characteristics?

- Do you believe that God put thought into your physical characteristics?

Developing a Healthy Body Image

A healthy body image combines acceptance of and respect for the body you have been given. It isn't a sense of pride, exactly; it is an agreement that God is the Potter and you are the clay. It is an ability to see beyond the world's message that "you are your body." A healthy body image enables you to celebrate that God made you and loves you.

- Do you think that God made a mistake when He gave you your body?

- Do you need to make peace with yourself and accept the parts of your body you cannot change?

> How does an unhealthy body image hold you back from what God wants for your life?

Steps to a Healthier Body Image

1. Identify the parts of your body you hate. Every woman has something that she dislikes about her body. Most women especially despise the area from the waist to the thighs.

> What bothers you the most about your body?

2. Identify why you began to hate those parts. When I talk to parents about helping their children have healthy body images, I often specifically address fathers of adolescent daughters. I have counseled many women with unhealthy body images who heard in their formative years negative words from fathers—words that subconsciously stuck with them all their lives. A father's jaded remark cuts deeply into his daughter's sense of value. He might say, "Look at your big hips," or tease her about her bra size, and that does a lot of damage. Other people's comments may also contribute to reasons why a woman might hate her body.

> What can you remember about why you hate a certain part of your body?

3. Look at yourself in perspective. Since body image is what you think you look like on the outside, developing a healthy body image begins with healthy self-talk. In fact, negative body image is fueled by negative self-talk. This takes many forms. Exaggeration is by far the most common form of unhealthy self-talk that women use. In conversations with other women, we exaggerate our flaws in order to be accepted. We believe the world's philosophy that we should all be thin and beautiful. We reject our positive features as we focus on our negative ones. We think others are as obsessed with our flaws as we are.

❧ In what ways or in what situations do you exaggerate your body flaws?

4. Develop an awareness of your positive features. God has given each of us gifts and talents to build up the body of Christ. Our physical bodies house those talents and gifts. We need to take account of our positive features. Do you have pretty eyes? What is it you like best about the body God gave you?

Women with unhealthy body images focus on one or two flaws even though they may have several attractive characteristics.

❧ What is it you like the most about your body?

5. Change what you can change and accept what you can't change. If you don't like certain features about yourself, try to do the best you can with what you have. Use tasteful makeup and clothes to present yourself in a way that makes you comfortable. We do feel better when we are pleased with the way we look. But it is equally important to keep this in balance. An example of this is cosmetic surgery. Many people who have cosmetic surgery feel better about themselves for a short time before returning to a negative self-image. The problem isn't with what is wrong on the outside; it's with what is wrong on the inside.

Make the changes that help you deemphasize negative features and emphasize the positive aspects of your body and appearance. The goal is to be free from preoccupation with your appearance and free to live your life.

❧ What efforts do you make to look your best?

6. Keep growing and developing Christlikeness. As you grow in your relationship with Christ, life takes on a whole new perspective. The diameter of your thighs fades in importance. Some of the parts of your body that you have disliked so intensely hardly seem worth a thought. Perhaps there are some body parts for which you'll give thanks.

A woman who has an anchor for her soul is not easily tossed about by an overemphasis on her body and appearance.

❧ How can you keep your body image healthy so you are free to do God's work?

Our Sexuality and Our Bodies

At first I didn't intend to include a chapter on body image or sex. But when I was teaching this material to a group of women, many of their questions at the end of our time together helped me see how a discussion of our feminine identity leads us directly to many questions about the physical aspects of femininity. In the world, femininity means sexuality. Our culture insists that the more sex appeal we have, the more feminine we are. That simply is not true.

Sex and the Christian woman seem to be mutually exclusive topics. Although God is not a sexual being, He did create us to be that way. In fact, sex is a metaphor for the key issues we have been talking about. In the sex act, a woman is warm and receiving, while a man must be strong and penetrating. Both the oneness God wants for our relationships and the differences required to create oneness are reflected in the act of intercourse.

The moment sin entered the world, our sexuality underwent enormous changes. In Genesis 2:24-25, Adam and Eve's nakedness produced no shame. But in Genesis 3:7, sexuality instantly became a matter of confusion and fear. For Adam and Eve, the first effect of sin was a desire to hide their sexuality. At some point, we all face a similar sense of shame about our sexuality. No one is immune from this.

Darlene still cringes from the severe shame she felt the day her mother walked into her bedroom to find Darlene and her four-year-old male neighbor with their pants off examining each other's body parts. Her mother's face and angry reaction still haunt her to this day. Darlene needed her mother to teach her and her friend that this was not the best way to learn about their differences. They needed to be taught that they should not undress in front of each other but that their curiosity about their differences was natural. Her mother could have recognized that this was a good time to talk to Darlene about the differences between boys and girls—a characteristic curiosity of four year olds.

What does a wise father tell his son about sex? Proverbs 5:18-19 says, "Let your fountain be blessed, and rejoice with the wife of your youth. As a loving deer and a graceful doe, let her breasts satisfy you at all times; and always be enraptured with her love (NKJV)." Those are the words of King Solomon giving instruction to his son about life and sex. Even after the Fall, God wanted us to celebrate our sexuality. He designed the fullest expression of our sexuality to be experienced in marriage. Sex distinguishes the marriage relationship from all others, because it is in this relationship alone that God desires us to relate sexually with our marriage partner.

> [12]"Everything is permissible for me"—but not everything is
> beneficial. "Everything is permissible for me"—but I will
> not be mastered by anything. [13]"Food for the stomach and
> the stomach for food"—but God will destroy them both.
> The body is not meant for sexual immorality, but for the
> Lord, and the Lord for the body. [14]By his power God raised
> the Lord from the dead, and he will raise us also. [15]Do you
> not know that your bodies are members of Christ himself?
> Shall I then take the members of Christ and unite them
> with a prostitute? Never! [16]Do you not know that he who
> unites himself with a prostitute is one with her in body?
> For it is said, "The two will become one flesh." [17]But he
> who unites himself with the Lord is one with him in spirit.
> [18]Flee from sexual immorality. All other sins a man commits
> are outside his body, but he who sins sexually sins against
> his own body. [19]Do you not know that your body is a
> temple of the Holy Spirit, who is in you, whom you have
> received from God? You are not your own; [20]you were

bought at a price. Therefore honor God with your body (1 Corinthians 6:12-20).

- What does it mean that the body is not meant for sexual immorality?
- Why does Satan constantly try to get us to use our bodies this way?
- What is the body meant for, according to verses 13 and 20?
- What happens to our bodies if we use them for sexual immorality?
- What is different about the sin of sexual immorality?
- What is the body, according to verse 19?
- What does it mean that your body is the temple of God?

God created you as a sexual being, but He did not create you for sexual immorality. When you use your sexuality in immoral ways, you hurt your body, mind, and soul. Satan constantly tempts you toward sexual immorality because He knows it will disrupt your relationship with God. Our bodies were meant for God and to use to honor God. When you sin sexually, you sin against yourself. Your body is the temple of the Holy Spirit, allowing you to take God with you everywhere you go.

- Who designed sex? What are characteristics of healthy sex, according to Proverbs 5:18-19? (Refer back to page 132.)

Sex and the Married Woman

We live in such a sex-craving society that we are often left wondering whether we are missing out on something special because we are Christ's.

God, our Creator, designed sex for married couples (Genesis 2:24-25), and He designed it to be wonderfully pleasurable (Proverbs 5:18-19). The kind of sex the world entices us with focuses on physical pleasure. The kind of sex that God speaks about is also pleasurable, but it is so much more than that. Sexual encounters flowing out of a relationship founded on love and commitment enrich and increase emotional as well as physical intimacy.

God designed sex to be an enriching part of our journey to intimacy. The kind of sex exploited in the tabloids and talk shows is one thing; the kind of sex God created us to enjoy in a committed, monogamous, and meaningful relationship is quite another. This is especially true for women. For a woman to enjoy and find deeper pleasure in sexual intimacy, she must feel safe in the arms of her lover. That's where the monogamous, committed part comes in. A man is also free to discover the delight of satisfying the wife of his youth when he commits to sex God's way.

Sex can't fix a marriage, and it isn't the center of a good one, but it does help us enjoy marriage more. As we anchor our marriage and commitment to each other in Christ, we find that sexual intimacy is the icing on the cake. In reality, sexual intimacy is good for you. The hormones that are released during sexual intercourse fight depression, strengthen the immune system, and decrease heart attacks.

Sex and the Single Woman

Sexuality for the single Christian woman is an equally perplexing plight. Though she has no partner with whom to enjoy, explore, and engage her sexual side, she has feelings, urges, and hormones with which to contend.

Single Christian women struggle with their sexuality in different ways. Some are virgins—seeming aliens in today's world. Others may have had sex with one man before being divorced or widowed. Still other single women have had multiple partners.

Our sexuality emphasizes our loneliness. All women struggle with loneliness, but the single woman faces a different kind of loneliness. If she is struggling to trust God's desire that she not engage in sexual encounters outside of marriage, she may feel left out of something important. She is, after all, a sexual being, so when she isn't being sexual, she feels that a part of her isn't even alive.

The grass always seems greener on the other side. I know married women who are experiencing the physical act of intercourse and yet are living with a deadness in their souls. I also know married women who dread that act of sex because of what it represents to them. They may be envious of single women, who are not expected to be sexual.

Henri Nouwen wrote: "It is obvious that our brokenness is often most painfully experienced with respect to our sexuality. . . . Our sexuality reveals to us our enormous yearning for communion."[5]

That yearning for communion, for oneness, can sometimes lead a woman down the wrong path and into sexual sin. What then? In 1 Corinthians 6:18 we are told, "Flee immorality. Every other sin that a man commits is outside the body, but the immoral man sins against his own body" (NASB).

It takes just as much grace to cover our sins against our bodies as it does sins committed against others. Sin is sin to God, and grace is the antidote. That grace is possible only because of Jesus' supreme sacrifice—becoming sin for us so we could receive His grace. Sexual sin hits us hard emotionally in part because it is so personal, by far the most intimate of sins. We carry the effects of that kind of sin with us because it affects our bodies. We can't get away from it because it may awaken even more desires to overrule our decisions or leave behind sexually transmitted diseases, pregnancy, or loss of relationship. It is difficult to separate sin entered into with the body from one's essential self.

Sexual Abuse and Sexuality

Many women have been used sexually. There is a difference between what our justice system considers sexual abuse and what our souls consider sexual abuse. As I help women understand their femininity,

I broaden the definition of sexual abuse from being touched in sexual areas and forced to have intercourse to include other inappropriate sexual messages and intrusions as well.

There is a correlation in the soul between sexuality and identity. The physical sensations resulting from being sexually violated range from feeling nothing to feeling slight pleasure to feeling pain. All do damage. If the woman feels pleasure, she invariably feels guilty and may even think she caused the abuse. If a woman feels nothing, it is because she has disassociated from her body—which is not good in itself—and she also feels she is wrong. If she experiences pain, it is because the perpetrator is hurting her body. But the greater damage is done to the emotions.

Emotionally, the woman feels sick, used, and dirty. She develops a core belief that something about her is wrong and that is why the abuse occurred. Many times she takes her bad feelings out on her own body. She might gain a lot of weight as a way to avoid relationships with men. She might become bulimic or anorexic. She may feel suicidal and depressed because she represses her anger and feelings of disgust for fear of experiencing even greater pain and rejection.

The greatest damage she can do is to cut herself off from her soul. In effect, she commits emotional suicide, believing that if she lets herself feel at all, she will only feel pain. In this way she becomes disconnected from her love needs, and that, in turn, disconnects her from God and others.

- How do you feel about your body and your sexuality?

- Do you trust God's plan for your sexuality?

How we view our bodies and our sexuality says a lot about our trust in God. Do you trust that God made you? I think we could each wear one of those tags that sometimes come on garments or handbags: "The material used to manufacture this garment is uniquely designed. Any flaws that appear are part of the unique quality and are not considered flaws in the material." Do you trust God that the full expression of your sexuality should be reserved for a monogamous, committed, married relationship? He tells you that only because He loves you. Learn to trust the God who made you. Accept the feminine physique He gave you. Rejoice in being the temple of the Holy Spirit. Treat yourself with respect and dignity.

Discussion Questions

1. Does God care about how we feel about our bodies?
2. Why should we keep our bodies healthy?
3. How does obsessing about body flaws keep us from serving God with our bodies?
4. Why did God create sex?
5. How does sexual immorality hurt us in a different way from other sins?
6. How does God want us to feel about our bodies?

Chapter Eleven

A Woman After God's Own Heart

A lot of little girls begin planning their weddings as young children. They think about the dresses they will wear. They talk about the appearance of their grooms. They look to marriage as a kind of redemption. After all, once Snow White and Cinderella found their princes and were married, everyone lived happily ever after. The only reality that can spoil that little-girl notion is a couple of years of marriage itself. Planning a wedding requires a lot of work, but marriage requires even more.

There is another wedding feast to which we can look forward. It is a wedding in which we are not only the person being honored but also the invited guest. We are each invited to be the bride of Christ. But being the bride of Christ does not require all the work and effort asked of a bride on earth. We are invited to the wedding feast of the Lamb. All that needs to be done has been done for us.

My mother made my wedding dress. It was beautiful and took many hours to complete. As the bride of Christ, my wedding dress is taken care of by the Groom. We each will wear His robes of righteousness, woven for us by His sacrificial gift—His own life. We women (and men) often don't realize what is promised to us. There will be a point in time when God will be able to love us as completely as He desires. He will bring us, the church, to Christ, our Groom.

With the divorce rate on the rise and love for a lifetime being seen as an out-of-date notion, the full beauty of the metaphor of a wedding and God's love for us is obscured. On earth, a wedding is the hope of hopes. We are each hoping to find the relationship that will heal us, that will complete us. We are all hoping that we will discover the one person who will love us unconditionally. But whether we ever marry on earth or not, there is a Groom who is waiting patiently to celebrate His love for us the way He desires. Before Jesus left this earth, He instituted the sacrament of the wine and bread. (Refer to Luke 22:15-16 on page 127.)

❧ When did Jesus say He would eat this again?

He told the disciples that He would not eat of the wine and bread until we are reunited with Him in heaven. He is a Groom greater than all grooms, the true love of our life. And best of all, He is willing to wait for us.

If you are like me, you are eager for that wedding feast to take place. You long to be loved the way you were created to be loved, with no obstacles or misunderstandings. In my anticipation for that wedding to take place, I've noticed something. It is the patience of the Groom. Generation after generation passes on this earth, and still our Groom waits for His special celebration. Brian and I were engaged for eight months, and that seemed an eternity. Jesus has been waiting nearly 2,000 years. Why is He so patient?

Several things are clear: One is that Jesus loves us. The second is that God has a plan. God lets us know about the wedding feast, but the day and hour it will occur are not for us to know.

> No one knows about that day or hour, not even the angels in heaven, nor the Son, but only the Father (Matthew 24:36).

❧ Does Jesus know the day of this great reunion?

God tells us how He wants to love us then, when there are no barriers of sin, so that we will desire to respond to His love now. Not even Jesus knows the day and the hour of our reunion with Him.

I think of my years on earth as an opportunity to discover the love of God in a unique way. I know He loves me, and I know what He has planned for me. But it seems that He also has given me these years on earth to discover His love even in uncomfortable living conditions. Might this be like an earthly marriage? I know couples who begin their marriages having it all. The bride has a Jaguar in the driveway, takes fabulous trips, and owns a beautiful home. None of it guarantees a good marriage. You cannot buy happiness. It is a gift. If God gave me everything I wanted instantly, He couldn't teach me about what I really want.

I hope that you are closer to receiving your true identity and accepting who you really are. King David was a man who had a clear sense of who he was. Yes, he failed to live up to all the commands God gave him; he did give in to sin and compromise. But one thing is clear: he was a man after God's own heart. In 1 Samuel 13:14 Samuel said of David, "the Lord has sought out a man after his own heart . . ." That description of David makes me think that he enjoyed an intimate relationship with God.

❧ How would you describe the intimacy between God and David?

❧ What do you think God meant when He described David as a man after God's own heart?

If you are going to be a woman after God's own heart, you must first know His heart. Perhaps you have a friend, mother, husband, or boyfriend who is special to you. You know what is most important to her or him. People will often call me to ask what kind of gift my husband, Brian, might like. They know that I know his heart and they trust I would know best what would make him happy. God is generous to tell us what is most important to Him. We don't have to search and wonder. He spells out what is in His heart for us.

> Love the Lord your God with all your heart and with all your soul and with all your strength (Deuteronomy 6:5).

❧ What does it mean to love God with all your heart? All your soul? All your strength?

Can you love God with your strength and not your heart? I think the Pharisees loved God that way. Can you love God with your soul and not your heart or strength? You can practice religious activity, but not with a heart that is set on loving God. Loving God with your heart, soul, and strength is what is required to genuinely love God.

There's something else that God wants us to know about His heart. He isn't just a self-glorifying God who wants us to show utter and complete devotion to Him. He longs to reward us.

> 35"Be dressed ready for service and keep your lamps burning, 36like men waiting for their master to return from a
> wedding banquet, so that when he comes and knocks they
> can immediately open the door for him. 37It will be good
> for those servants whose master finds them watching
> when he comes. I tell you the truth, he will dress himself
> to serve, will have them recline at the table and will come
> and wait on them. 38It will be good for those servants
> whose master finds them ready, even if he comes in the
> second or third watch of the night. 39But understand this:

> If the owner of the house had known at what hour the thief was coming, he would not have let his house be broken into. [40]You also must be ready, because the Son of Man will come at an hour when you do not expect him" (Luke 12:35-40).

- Why would the master be pleased to find his servants waiting at all hours for his return?

- What does the master do in response to his servants' devotion?

- What would motivate a master to respond this way?

- Do you know many masters who respond this way?

- Do you think God really wants to respond this way to us, His faithful servants?

Would you expect a master who comes home to find his servants faithfully fulfilling their duties in his absence to sit down and serve them in return? I know I wouldn't. I would think the master would be pleased, reward them, maybe; but serve them? Out of the question.

- Remember what Jesus did in John 13:1-17 when He washed the disciples' feet? How is He like the master He described in Luke 12?

Jesus started out the very traditional Passover meal in a less-than-traditional way. He startled the disciples when He took off His outer garment, put on a servant's garb, and washed their feet. Later He explained that this was an object lesson. It was a picture of how He expected them to lead after He was gone.

Read the description God gave us through John in Revelation 22:12-14.

> [12]"Behold, I am coming soon! My reward is with me, and I will give to everyone according to what he has done. [13]I am the Alpha and the Omega, the First and the Last, the Beginning and the End. [14]"Blessed are those who wash their robes, that they may have the right to the tree of life, and may go through the gates into the city.

How does this reveal the heart of God for us, His daughters?

He can't wait to welcome us home, and He has great plans for us. They are plans that we are going to love!

Becoming a Woman After God's Own Heart

The Westminster Catechism says that the chief end of man is to glorify God and enjoy Him forever. When I think about this, I see how glorifying God saves me from myself. I realize that if I am glorifying God, I am not glorifying myself. When I glorify myself, I often hurt others in the process. This world was created to be in balance. It is only when God is in His rightful place as the center of our lives that we live in balance. God rescues me from existing to glorify myself because this position damages me and others. It is only when I seek to glorify God that harmony is created.

My hope for my life on earth is to become a woman after God's own heart. I want to respond to His love and to experience as much of it as I can while I live here. What does it mean be a woman after God's own heart?

1. A woman after God's own heart accepts God's purposes. We've already spent quite some time on why and how we women try to control our relationships. The change that takes place in our hearts when our hearts are set on God is that we yield our will to His. In essence, we stop demanding that all our needs be met while we are here on earth. We believe that God has a bigger plan. We trust Him. We let go and let God!

God's way is not that of a tyrant, demanding power and control. His way is that of love, always inviting us to ever-deepening intimacy. But we choose to go our own way. When we try to love our way—loving to get and loving to control—we end up loveless. One of the signs of the end times that Jesus mentioned is lovelessness. He said, "Because of the increase of wickedness, the love [agape] of most will grow cold . . ." (Matthew 24:12). Our souls are created for love, but this love can't exist without God, or it will be selfish and demanding. We must exchange our own way for God's way.

2. A woman after God's own heart is spiritually sensitive. God never grabs us by the shoulders and shakes us and threatens us into obedience. He powerfully but quietly draws us into deep relationship with Him. Discover an example of this by reading 1 Kings 19:9-13.

> [9]There he went into a cave and spent the night. And the
> word of the Lord came to him: "What are you doing
> here, Elijah?" [10]He replied, "I have been very zealous for
> the Lord God Almighty. The Israelites have rejected your
> covenant, broken down your altars, and put your
> prophets to death with the sword. I am the only one left,
> and now they are trying to kill me too." [11]The Lord said,
> "Go out and stand on the mountain in the presence of
> the Lord, for the Lord is about to pass by." Then a great
> and powerful wind tore the mountains apart and shat-
> tered the rocks before the Lord, but the Lord was not in
> the wind. After the wind there was an earthquake, but
> the Lord was not in the earthquake. [12]After the earth-
> quake came a fire, but the Lord was not in the fire. And
> after the fire came a gentle whisper. [13]When Elijah heard
> it, he pulled his cloak over his face and went out and
> stood at the mouth of the cave. Then a voice said to
> him, "What are you doing here, Elijah?"

❧ How did God not come to Elijah?

❧ How did God come to Elijah?

God was not in the great and powerful wind, God was not in the earthquake, and God was not in the fire. God spoke to Elijah in a gentle whisper.

I would never want to be one of those who reduces God to a tiny voice inside of me. Our God is much greater than that. But our God is one who gives us messages of His love and His righteousness daily. He speaks to us in a still, small voice. We must learn to be spiritually sensitive so we can recognize it.

God's voice is the one that exposes my sin yet always invites me to greatness. If you are listening to a voice that describes your failures again and again, you aren't hearing God.

God doesn't shout at us; He whispers our names. Do you hear Him? Do you sense Him calling you away from the world and the false hopes it gives us?

3. A woman after God's own heart is focused on loving others. The majority of Jesus' last words were instructions about loving one another. If you share the heart of God, you will discover a supernatural ability to love God's people.

> By this all men will know that you are my disciples, if you love one another (John 13:35).

❧ What is evidence that we are Christians?

Do you resemble God by the way that you love? Do others know you are a Christian by the love you show? Jesus says that other people should be able to recognize us as Christians by the evidence of our love for others (John 13:35).

I'm humbled by my lack of love even as I drive down the highway. In Dallas, I do a lot of driving. I feel as if I'm in competition with people to be the first in a lane, to make it through the yellow light, to find the lane that is moving the fastest. In the process, there is no love in my heart. I'm insulted by the guy who pulls into the insufficient space I left between me and the car in front so as to discourage cutters. When he pulls in anyway, and I have to touch my brakes, I'm shocked at the hatred seeping from my heart. Here I am, hating a person I don't even know, to whom I have never spoken, but who has delayed me just a little in getting to my destination.

God doesn't want me to be a petty driver, risking my life for a chance to be first. He wants so much more for me. He knows I can do better than that. He wants me to be like Him, to learn the freedom of loving others when there is no reason to love. Jesus had the audacity to instruct His disciples to love even their enemies (Matthew 5:44). Imagine that. Loving enemies!

Who benefits most when we follow God's path of love?

At first I thought it would be the person receiving the act of love. When I thought a little harder, I realized that when I love like that, I love like Jesus! I begin to resemble God again. I'm no longer angry when I choose to love. I'm free to give love because I have room in my heart to share.

This life of love is possible only by getting in touch with the One who truly loves us. The closer I get to God's heart, the more I want to love others. I long to love because I have been so deeply loved.

4. A woman after God's own heart finds comfort in God. We don't like to be in pain, and God doesn't like us to be in pain either. In fact, one of the descriptions of heaven is that there will be no more tears! It's not just a shampoo. How do we find comfort in God? Consider how David found that comfort in Psalm 23:4.

> Even though I walk through the valley of the shadow of death, I will fear no evil, for you are with me; your rod and your staff, they comfort me.

When I read the Psalms, I am amazed by David's willingness to receive God's comfort. He described situations much worse than I've ever had to endure. He spoke of being homeless, hungry, beaten up, and forsaken. But the end of every psalm describes how he received comfort. The comfort he received didn't come from a change in circumstances. In many of those psalms, David was being pursued by enemies who were trying to kill him, and he was still hiding out in caves and living like a madman. But he received comfort from God, who was always near. David found comfort in the assuring presence of God as he walked through his most frightening and dreaded experiences in life. The rod and staff are symbols for the Word of God and the Holy Spirit.

Jesus endured the shame and the discomfort of the cross. Think about the degree of discomfort Jesus endured for us, not only on the cross but also during His life on earth. For most of us, the discomfort He endured during infancy compares little with the pain we felt in childhood and adulthood. But consider being God and becoming human. It would be similar to you or me taking on the form of a cockroach. For God, just being human was uncomfortable.

5. A woman after God's own heart communicates soul to soul with God. Having a heart for God will transform your prayer life. Prayer becomes a vital and loving communication between two beings.

❧ Read the description of the early believers' prayer in Acts 4:24-31.

> [24]When they heard this, they raised their voices together in prayer to God. "Sovereign Lord," they said, "you made the heaven and the earth and the sea, and everything in them.

> [25]You spoke by the Holy Spirit through the mouth of your
> servant, our father David: " 'Why do the nations rage and
> the peoples plot in vain? [26]The kings of the earth take their
> stand and the rulers gather together against the Lord and
> against his Anointed One.' " [27]Indeed Herod and Pontius
> Pilate met together with the Gentiles and the people of
> Israel in this city to conspire against your holy servant Jesus,
> whom you anointed. [28]They did what your power and will
> had decided beforehand should happen. [29]Now, Lord, con-
> sider their threats and enable your servants to speak your
> word with great boldness. [30]Stretch out your hand to heal
> and perform miraculous signs and wonders through the
> name of your holy servant Jesus." [31]After they prayed, the
> place where they were meeting was shaken. And they were
> all filled with the Holy Spirit and spoke the word of God
> boldly.

❧ What happened after they prayed?

❧ Has that ever happened to you?

❧ How has prayer affected your life?

After this congregation of believers lifted their burden to work in God's spiritual kingdom, the Holy Spirit descended upon them in answer to their prayers. This was a very dramatic moment in Christian history. I have seen it repeated in a few church and Christian meetings that I have attended. There is nothing like recognizing the powerful presence of the Holy Spirit in response to a prayer.

> [26]In the same way, the Spirit helps us in our weakness. We
> do not know what we ought to pray for, but the Spirit
> himself intercedes for us with groans that words cannot
> express.

> [34]Who is he that condemns? Christ Jesus, who died—more than that, who was raised to life—is at the right hand of God and is also interceding for us (Romans 8:26, 34).

❧ Who intercedes for us?

Think about what happens when we pray. Father, Son, and Holy Spirit are all involved in conversation with us! Romans 8:34 says that Jesus Christ is sitting at the right hand of God interceding for us. We pray, and Jesus Himself tells God about us. Romans 8:26 says that the Holy Spirit also intercedes on our behalf, putting into words the thoughts and ideas that are too deep for us to understand or express.

The very act of prayer remains mysterious to me, though I can testify that it transforms my personality. It changes me from being self-centered, worried, and preoccupied to being loving, at peace, and centered. I have seen prayer do the same for others. I have witnessed prayer overcome anxiety, depression, despair, and desperation in the lives of people I counsel. Prayer changes the deepest gauges of our souls and somehow aligns them again so that our souls are free to know God's love.

6. A woman after God's own heart is deeply assured of God's love for her. Read 1 John 3:1.

> How great is the love the Father has lavished on us, that we should be called children of God! And that is what we are!

Keep reading it slowly, leaving the last word off each time until you say only the word "How." Pause for reflection each time you leave off a word.

❧ How do you feel after reading this scripture?

❧ Describe God's love for you in your journal. You could write a letter to yourself from God based on the principles you have learned in this study.

When my kids squabble, I am often summoned to the room. One may have said wrong words to the other or hit, pushed, or kicked the other. I remind the one, "Benjamin is God's son, and it is wrong for you to treat God's son that way." Or another time, I might say, "Rachel is my daughter. You should not call my daughter a name like that." Those words seem to get their attention. The value of their sibling is put into perspective.

This method works both ways. One day when I was yelling at Rachel for something she had done, she said to me, "I am God's daughter and you shouldn't talk to God's daughter like that."

I said, "You know, you are right."

I'm glad she's getting the picture. A woman after God's own heart knows Whose daughter she is. She doesn't mistreat herself or let others mistreat her. She realizes that she is special.

7. A woman after God's own heart changes her world. What were Christ's last instructions for the small band of believers before He ascended into heaven?

> 6So when they met together, they asked him, "Lord,
> are you at this time going to restore the kingdom to
> Israel?" 7He said to them: "It is not for you to know
> the times or dates the Father has set by his own author-
> ity. 8But you will receive power when the Holy Spirit
> comes on you; and you will be my witnesses in
> Jerusalem, and in all Judea and Samaria, and to the
> ends of the earth." 9After he said this, he was taken up
> before their very eyes, and a cloud hid him from their
> sight (Acts 1:6-9).

The believers needed to trust that the dates and times and plans of God had already been set for eternity. They were to wait until the time that the Holy Spirit came upon them, and then they were to be His witnesses all over the world.

- How did these precious ones gathered there do in carrying out His instructions?

- How are you doing in carrying forth His plan?

- How is this world a better place because of you?

Oliver Wendell Holmes said, "I find the greatest thing in this world is not so much where we stand as in what direction we are moving."[6] In what direction are you moving? Are you making a difference in the world? Some people are remembered for generations. Perhaps they founded a nation, painted a masterpiece, or were the first to walk on the moon. The vast majority of us, though, will wither like the grass and go unremembered after we die. But we are each given 70 to 80 years, God willing, to make a difference in the lives of the people with whom we share our planet.

God says that succeeding generations are punished for the sins of the fathers, yet His love is extended to many more generations of those who keep His commandments (Deuteronomy 5:9-10). So, although we may not be remembered, how we live will affect those who come after us—for good or for ill. How will you live your life on earth? Will you make a spiritual difference? Or will you commit sins that will affect generations to come?

God longs for you to know that you are His beloved daughter. He wants you to know who you are, who you were born to be, and how to enjoy the gift of the life He has given you.

Living for Jesus will mean swimming against the world's current. We may not find approval from our society. But so what?

We are the nurturers and helpers, the thinkers and peacemakers. We do and we make do. We bask in His love.

He made us and we are His. There is nothing like us!

Discussion Questions

1. How do we become women after God's own heart?

2. What are some of the characteristics you will see in a person who really knows God?

3. How have you come to know who you are through this study?

4. How have you seen God using you to change this world?

Appendix

Suggestions for Leaders

Getting Started

I'm glad that you have chosen to lead this group of women. I know you will be blessed by your efforts to serve God in this way. I recommend that you read the text and answer the questions of at least the first two chapters before you begin the study. You may choose to read through the entire book ahead of time, if you wish. The other women will be looking to you for guidance, and it is helpful if you have some familiarity with the book and its message.

You will be in charge of publicizing your study and inviting women to join your group. You will also organize the place, time, and dates of meetings.

The book is written to lead women in personal study of God's Word. You do not need to teach the material unless you choose to. The leader is a facilitator of discussion among the women. You do not have to be a Bible scholar to lead these discussions; you simply need to have a love for God, His Word, women, and ministry to be the perfect leader. You can best facilitate discussion by asking the questions and encouraging answers. Most of the questions ask for opinions and don't have a right or wrong answer. If there is any debate, the Bible is the supreme authority.

Publicity

You may be leading this study with a group that is already in existence, such as a book club, Sunday school class, or support group. In that case, the only publicity you will need to do is to announce the dates that you will begin the study and discuss how to purchase books.

If you are publicizing this study in your church, you should discuss the best ways to do this with your church staff. They will have an idea of how far in advance to begin publicity and how to handle sign-up. If you are meeting at the church, you will want to follow the procedures for reserving a room for your meeting. If your group meets in a home, you need to make those arrangements and include meeting times, dates, and places in the publicity.

The actual study involves 10 weeks. However, I suggest that you meet for 11 weeks if at all possible. When you meet for 11 weeks, it gives you the opportunity to have an introduction session that will set the tone for the rest of the study. I have found that it is helpful for individuals to know each other and have a sense of safety and fun in order for them to share openly. This is why an introduction session can be foundational to setting the tone of your meetings. In our busy world, many of us may see each other at church, yet know very little about one another.

Introduction Session

Get-Acquainted Activity

During the introduction session, it's helpful to have some kind of get-acquainted exercise. You could have each participant introduce herself by sharing her name, information about her family, and what she likes best about being a woman. You may want to use an exercise or game that you have enjoyed in the past and you think your group will respond well to.

Give an Overview of the Class

During the class, you as the leader need to provide an overview of the class, what participants can expect, what you have to offer, and why you are excited about beginning this study.

Encourage participants to come to the group discussions even if they haven't had time to read the material and answer the questions. Explain that they will get the most out of each lesson, however, if they have read the chapter and answered the individual questions before coming to class.

Clarify that during the class time, the group will go over the weekly discussion questions at the end of the chapter. The questions don't have to be done ahead of time.

Introduce the study and explain the logistics, including schedules of dates and the lesson that should be read, where to get a book, etc. It would be helpful to have a handout for each woman with the dates and chapters to be read.

Create an Atmosphere for Sharing

I find it helpful to create an atmosphere of sharing by setting some group rules:

- All sharing is voluntary.
- All comments shared will be kept confidential.
- We are here to love and support one another.

You could ask the group if they would like to add more rules and give their feedback.

As the leader, you might set the atmosphere by sharing your personal reflections on how you have come to know your true identity, either through reading this book or other experiences you have had. If you don't feel you've quite reached this goal, you might share where you are in your spiritual journey and what it is you hope to accomplish through doing this study.

Many leaders are afraid of silence. Give women time to share. Be sensitive to those who are reluctant to talk in groups by gently encouraging them to share. Don't let one woman dominate the whole discussion time.

Try not to put anyone on the spot or make her feel foolish for the response she gives.

I encourage you to pray for each participant. Ask God to give you the wisdom to lead the group. Again, most of the discussion questions don't have right or wrong answers, but if someone is saying something that contradicts Scripture, it is your responsibility to gently but firmly state the truth from Scripture. This is a lot of responsibility. But remember that the Holy Spirit is there to give you the wisdom you need.

Optional for First Session

Read the story *You Are Special* by Max Lucado (Wheaton: Good News Publishers, 1997). It provides a picture of the lesson each of us hopes to learn.

Discussion Questions

Go over the six discussion questions provided for the introduction session.

Closing

Close with prayer and an encouraging and enthusiastic attitude about beginning the next session.

Weeks 2–11

I recommend the following format for the rest of your sessions together.

You, as the leader, can welcome the group and set the tone for the rest of the meeting. Depending on your style, you may want to take a few minutes to share what you learned most from the week's lesson. A review time will help the women gather their thoughts and remember what they have studied so far. Then you may go directly to the discussion questions, or you may want to ask the women if there were any questions or comments they have from the lesson that they would like to ask or share with the class before you proceed to the discussion questions.

Prayer

There is a special intimacy that develops as women pray for each other. You can assign prayer partners or have a prayer list where women can share prayer requests. Women love to talk, so be sensitive to the best way to facilitate prayer in your group. You may want to have a list where they can write their requests and make copies right after the study for women to take home and pray for.

I want to personally thank you for the gift you are giving to God and these women you serve through your leadership. Blessings to you.

Notes

Chapter 6

1. Walter Wangerin, *As For Me and My House* (Nashville: Thomas Nelson, 1987), p. 79.
2. C. S. Lewis, ed., *George MacDonald: An Anthology* (London: Geoffrey Bles, 1970), p. 26.
3. Walter A. Henrichsen, *Disciples Are Made, Not Born* (Wheaton, Ill.: Victor, 1978), p. 16.

Chapter 8

3. Jeanne Guyon, *Experiencing the Depths of Christ,* (Camp Hill, PA: Christian Publications, 1981), p. 27.

Chapter 9

4. Gary Smalley and John Trent, *The Hidden Value of a Man* (Colorado Springs, Colo.: Focus on the Family, 1992), p. 91.

Chapter 10

5. Henri Nouwen, *Life of the Beloved* (New York: Crossroad, 1992), p. 73.

Chapter 11

6. Oliver Wendell Holmes, cited in *Guideposts* (August 1996), p. 62.